TONGUES & TOTEMS

COMPARATIVE ARTS OF THE PACIFIC BASIN

A comparison of Northwest Coast Indian art with art forms of other cultures around the Pacific Basin, with special reference to the collection of the Alaska International Art Institute.

by starr & richard davis

ALASKA INTERNATIONAL ART INSTITUTE

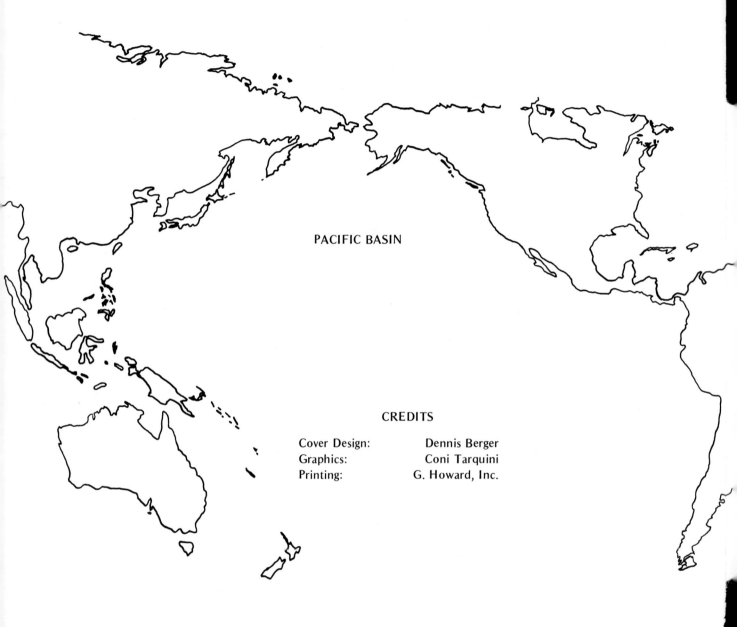

PACIFIC BASIN

CREDITS

Cover Design: Dennis Berger
Graphics: Coni Tarquini
Printing: G. Howard, Inc.

Alaska International Art Institute
3003 Wendy Way, Anchorage, Alaska 99503

CONTENTS

1. Left: Starr Davis, curator, standing in front of the Tsimshian totem carved by the tribe's chief, William Jeffrey, and designed by his daughter, Princess Little Ice. Mrs. Davis is holding a wood carving from the AIAI collection reminiscent of the great cosmic idol of Bolivia.

2. Right: Sketch of the Alaska International Art Institute, AIAI, by R. E. Cupp.

3. Far Right: Founder of the AIAI, Mrs. H. "Wendy" Jones examining the totem pole of Eagle and Whale, part of the collection.

4

The Alaska International Art Institute (AIAI) is the unique setting for Wendy Jones' personal art collection. Within this lively institute, fine arts, crafts, music, writing and dance are created and savored amidst comfortable furnishings, often a hearty fire, and a lovely view of Jones Lake mirroring Sitka spruce and mountains beyond. In this setting the art works seem not so much on display, but at home. Following the trail of Captain Cook, Wendy gathers art works on her world travels, and often intrigues visitors by relating the adventure behind each acquisition. It is her dream that the Institute should serve as a catalyst for cultural growth in Anchorage.

Five buildings of the AIAI, each shaped to its own character, contain all of Wendy's treasures:

1 — The A-frame: Alaskan and European works.
2 — Chapel of the Madonnas.
3 — Alaskan Studio.
4 — Oriental and Asian Exhibit.
5 — International Doll House.

4. MAP OF PACIFIC BASIN
with names of cultures mentioned in this book

SIBERIA

Old Bering Sea Culture
Chukchi Peninsula

Ghilyak

CHINA

Shang Dynasty (Honan Province)

Chou Dynasty

Ainu Culture, Hokkaido Isle

JAPAN

ALASKA

Pt. Hope
Koyukuk River
Kuskowim (Eskimo)
Anchorage
Prince Rupert
Haida

Tlingit
Tsimshian
Kwakiutl
Nootka   Salish
Vancouver Island

NORTHWEST COAST

U.S.A.

Zuni
Hopi Sinkyaki
Navajo   Mimbres
San Miguel de Allende
Tenochtitlan (Aztec) Teotihuacan (Mayan)
Monte Alban (Zapotec) Campeche Coast (Mayan)
El Meson (Mayan) Quirigua (Mayan)
Chiapas (Mayan)

Uxa Valley
Co
(Cuna)

Las Islands
(Cuna)

PANAMA

Costa Rica
Nicoya

MEXICO

PERU
Pacasmayo (Chimu)
Trujillo

Lake
Titicaca

Paracas

BOLIVIA
Tiahuanaco

Marquesas Islands

Sepik River
NEW GUINEA

New Ireland

New Britain

New Hebrides

New Caledonia

AUSTRALIA

Sumatra

Maori

NEW ZEALAND

6

ARTISTIC SIMILARITIES BETWEEN CULTURES: SOME THEORIES

During the year that I conducted tours through the Alaska International Art Institute, I began to search out relationships among the pieces of this diverse collection. Particularly, I came to use Northwest Coast Indian art as a basis for comparison with art forms from elsewhere in the "Pacific Basin" —— an arc more than 10,000 miles in length, ranging from the west coast of the Americas, past China, Japan, and coastal Siberia all the way to New Guinea and New Ireland (see map, p. 6). Despite the heterogeneous cultures and environments and the vast distances involved, and the likelihood that no two objects share the same date of creation, some intriguing resemblances began to emerge. The following list corresponds more or less with the structure of this book and indicates similarities among art objects from highly divergent cultures within the Pacific Basin.

Resemblances among art objects from Pacific Basin cultures —

design elements

1) Curvilinear, stylized rendition of human and animal forms; avoidance of botanical or landscape-related forms.

2) Tendency toward filling up "empty" space through:
- Symmetry of whole design.
- Bilateral split of a three-dimensional figure (laid out flat like a bear skin rug).
- Space fillers.
- Exaggeration or distortion.
- X-ray vision, joint marks.

cultural-visual motifs

3) Similar motifs:
- Splayed figure.
- Bird-reptile.
- Double-headed serpent.
- Protruding tongue.
- Bird-man.
- Totem pole.
- Step motif; fret hook.

4) Mythological elements: rebirth; transformation; dualism.

In addition to these visual or cultural parallels, anthropologists point out some "universal" features considered common to all primitive art. One is that the objects are made of available raw materials, each of which has its limitations and tends to produce a type: paint produces flat art; a wood-rich culture will tend to produce pole-shaped objects, etc.

ARTISTIC SIMILARITIES BETWEEN CULTURES: SOME THEORIES

Some similarities which crop up in apparently unrelated cultures may thus be accounted for. Another universal aspect of art from non-literate and pre-literate cultures seems to be the storing of information. A Northwest Coast totem pole, for instance, through its series of animal representations, brings to mind the legends and traditions of a given clan. Such knowledge is vital to the ordering of society and of man/nature relationships.

As can be seen by browsing through the pages of this book, the similarities outlined above occur in objects from cultures separated in both space and time by huge gulfs. **Do the resemblances spring from "independent invention," or are they due to cultural diffusion —the transfer of an element from one culture to another?** A long-standing and sometimes acrid debate has centered around this issue. The "diffusionists" are struck by visual and formal relationships, sometimes quite complex, which they feel must be more than coincidental. They attribute the resemblances to a remarkably widespread cross-cultural borrowing of artistic devices and techniques and even of mythological motifs and legends. Heine-Geldern* conjectured that these elements spread from an "Old Pacific Style" from China throughout the Pacific Basin (see diagram, p. 9).

Many anthropologists, though, admonish us not to apply the diffusionist concept too sweepingly. Claude Levi-Strauss** suggests that if historical evidence for diffusion is lacking, we might look for underlying "internal" or "psychological" connections to account for the outward similarities in art objects.[1] He goes on to remark that even if a diffusionist explanation is valid, we would still confront a basic problem: "Why should a cultural trait that has been borrowed or diffused through a long historical period remain intact? Stability is no less mysterious than change."[2] Accounting for why a given trait **hasn't** changed, after transmission through time or across cultures, may be as difficult as proving the cultural indebtedness in the first place. He concludes that if diffusion can be demonstrated, "it would not be a diffusion of details . . . but a diffusion of organic wholes wherein style, esthetic conventions, and religion are structurally related."[3]

Our intent is not to resolve this difference of opinion, though advocates of independent invention may find our focus on **comparisons** necessarily slighting their view. We would like to explore, with the reader, the resemblances found among objects in the AIAI collection, and to bring in enough additional examples from other sources to amplify and clarify. We hope you will enjoy the journey.†

---

* Robert Heine-Geldern, Professor Emeritus of the Ethnology, Pre-history and Art History of Asia at the University of Vienna, and the leading spokesman for the diffusionists.

** Claude Levi-Strauss, influential French structural anthropologist.

† Footnotes of an informational nature which supplement the text are indicated by asterisks. Footnotes intended as documentation have been placed in the "Footnotes" section, pp. 116 – 118, and are indicated numerically.

5. "DIFFUSIONIST" THEORY
(According to Heine-Geldern)

DNIESTRO-DANUBIAN STYLE

The Bronze Age style from southwest Russia, Romania, Transylvania, and the north Balkans. Represented by spiral motifs and bronze-castings. Came to China probably about 1800 B.C.

"OLD PACIFIC STYLE"

The probable native style of east Asia (3rd millennium B.C. or before), represented by totemic posts, bilateral representation (and perhaps "hockers").

SHANG STYLE

Early Bronze Age of north China. 1700–1100 B.C.

EARLY CHOU STYLE

Result of the amalgamation of Shang style and local elements from west China. 1100–750 B.C.

LATE CHOU STYLE

Early Chou with later Danubian and Caucasian elements. 750–200 B.C.

DONGSON STYLE

Bronze Age of southeast Asia, with local styles of Indochina. 750 B.C.–A.D. 100.

Widespread influences in Malaysia, Melanesia, and Polynesia, reaching the Americas through various channels and at various times. Examples:

Batak of Sumatra
Toradja of Celebes
Alor, Tinambar

Dyak of Borneo, Massin of east New Guinea, Ngada of Flores Island, Maori of New Zealand

Marquesas Islands

Western South America

Tajin style of Mexico
Ulua style of Honduras

Northwest Coast art
Amazon basin style
Cuna of Panama, etc.

 THE NORTHWEST COAST INDIANS

6. Tsonoqoa Mask.
    Kwakiutl, Northwest Coast.
    Wood, paint: turquoise, black, deep red; human hair.
    Tsonoqoa is a vain and clumsy giantess, a cannibal woman of the woods, who scares children into staying near home. She is usually represented as asleep. At ceremonies, dressed in a complete bearskin covering, her impersonator gropes his way along a rope leading to her seat.
    A family that wrested Tsonoqoa's secrets from her found that she controls the water of life, and brings wealth and good fortune. Decorating the inside of her house are many treasures of Sisiutl, an indication of her supernatural importance.[1]

Since Northwest Coast Indian art serves as the basis for comparison in this book, the reader might appreciate knowing something of its geographical and cultural background.

The Northwest Coast of North America includes the coastlines of Washington, British Columbia, and southern Alaska. Fig. 9 shows the tribal distribution.* Along this island-protected shore, beside fresh water streams, the people built their large winter lodges. To adorn them they transformed huge cedar logs from the verdant forests into handsomely carved and meaningfully decorated house posts and totem poles. (Figs. 105 and 106). Inside the lodges could be found utensils like storage boxes, dishes and ladles. Objects from the smallest spoon to a house front were distinctively carved with the clan's own totem-animal or clan-legend——reminders of the supernatural forces which lay beneath everyday existence. Colors were subtle, conservative, and until European contact were sparingly used. Pigments came from ochre and cinnabar (reds), soot (black), copper salts (green); these were made usable by mixing with saliva and salmon eggs. Brushes were made of porcupine guard hairs set in a wooden handle slit down the middle.

How long have Northwest Coast peoples been there? Evidence of their cultural development before the arrival of European explorers has been hard to come by. Prodigious rainfall and moisture rapidly decompose materials which might leave an archeological record. But at one site a combination of geological events and ingenious research techniques has greatly expanded our fragmentary knowledge. Near Neah Bay, a few miles south of Juan de Fuca Strait in Washington, a Nootka settlement now known as Ozette was engulfed from time to time by mud slides. The effect was similar to that of the volcanic action at Pompeii: decay was drastically retarded and houses, tools, containers and art work were preserved in a thick layer of clay. Since 1966 a special water spray technique has been used to remove the layers, revealing an occupancy of several thousand years. The director of the project, Richard D. Daugherty, considers the find "the most complete archaeological

---

* Northwest Coast (NWC) tribes include the Tlingit, Tsimshian, and Haida in the north; the Kwakiutl and Bella Coola in the central section; and the Nootka, Salish and Quilliute in the south. Although these tribes have many cultural and artistic elements in common, they have distinct social, stylistic and linguistic differences. These, however, lie largely outside the scope of this book.

record of Northwest Coast Indian culture" ever discovered.[2] The box shown in Fig. 7 was taken from this site. Though its precise age has not been determined,* its typical NWC features (curvilinear style and thick eyebrows) provide a solid clue as to the long history of the region's artistic traditions.** Captain Cook, who visited the Nootka in 1778, provides us with further evidence of their cultural vitality. "Everything was ornamented," he wrote, "in their kind of frieze work." Clearly the richness of their artistic production impressed him, and can be seen in the samples he took which today reside in the British Museum in London.

Within a very few years after Captain Cook's visit, European explorers and traders were combing the waters of this region for the tremendous potential of seal and sea otter furs, a resource which they soon managed to deplete. The full impact of the white man's economy on the cultural and artistic life of the native peoples was yet to be felt.

7.   **Large Wooden Box**
Wakashan Culture,
Ozette, Northwest Coast, 1400 A.D.
Wood, paint, sea otter teeth.

Religious life among Northwest Coast peoples was dominated by belief in supernatural forces, which were thought to underlie the events of everyday existence. So intimate was this relationship that the spirit-world was not perceived as far removed from the ordinary, external world. Through contact with the supernatural, phenomena such as the fluctuation of the tides and the salmon run could be explained; and the spirits which controlled every animate existence might give aid if properly approached. In achieving this purpose, an important mediating force was the shaman. A shaman (or "medicine man") was an important if eccentric member of the community. As evidence of his unique rapport and healing powers he would perform dances using an assortment of objects such as masks, costumes, rattles and charms, all carved of wood and beautifully designed. Many of these now occupy a prominent place in museum collections. (See Figs. 40 and 41.)

---

*   It is thought to be about 500 years old, dating from the time of the most massive mudslide.

**   It is also speculated that the northern tribes migrated from the Kamchatka Peninsula around 1000 A.D., greatly enriching and influencing the art of the area.

An even more pervasive manifestation of supernatural belief was **totemism:** "an association between groups of people and some animal, plant or inanimate object."[3] In the northern part of the region the totem, or guardian spirit, became a "family crest figure acquired by inheritance; while in the central region, among the Kwakiutl, initiation into the secret societies was a kind of collective spirit quest."*[4] In the north an animal such as the Raven, Bear, Eagle, or Thunderbird became a totem for a clan, and was a principal element of the geneology depicted in clan objects such as "totem"** poles. The totem animal decoratively identified all carved objects from the great communal houses to an ordinary fishing hook.

Before European contact, the NWC social hierarchy consisted largely of chiefs, freemen and slaves, all of whom engaged in a complex hunting-and-gathering economy. Resources were abundant, but by no means inexhaustible as some anthropologists assumed.[5] Environmental variations may have caused temporary scarcity of subsistence goods in some areas, while normal conditions prevailed not too far away. One response to such imbalance was warfare. Another more socially acceptable means of relieving the demographic pressure was the potlatch.

8. "Off to the Potlatch"
    Oil painting by Sydney Laurence around 1928.
    Colors: blues, grey, white, yellow, red.
    Poster for the Northern Pacific Railway.

The potlatch was a tremendous feast given by a chief to celebrate a social function such as the birth of a son, the construction of a totem pole or house, or the validation of a right. The pre-contact potlatch served somewhat the same role as a legal document: by eating the host's food and accepting his gifts, the guests accepted his claims and formally agreed to respect them. During the event, which could last several days, impressive, drama-

---

*   In the south, however, the guardian spirit "was considered a personal possession, to be acquired by the individual in a solitary quest of his own."[6]

**   Strict anthropological usage limits the term "totem" to a pole containing totemic elements belonging only to a given clan; whereas a NWC totem pole may illustrate the clan's owner, its rival, or events in a myth.

tic performances of family legends were given by masked and costumed dancers (Fig. 87), silhouetted against a flickering fire. Gifts were ostentatiously and ceremoniously exchanged. Elaborate, year-long preparation preceded the occasion, and included the amassing of huge quantities of food and materials. Guests, too, loaded their canoes with prized possessions and came from miles away. (Fig. 8). Not surprisingly, artistic production was an intimate part of all this activity. Elaborate wood carvings of high quality were commissioned by the chief, and the best artists received rewards commensurate to those Matisse or Picasso commanded in their time.

Interpretations of the potlatch differ. Until recently, most analysts have emphasized the obsessive quest for prestige which seemed to motivate the ceremony. The intense rivalries of the potlatch, so the theory goes, grow out of an economy of overabundance and a surplus of spare time. The goal of the occasion was for the host to impress his guests, and acquire prestige for himself, by showering them with more gifts than they could repay. Their failure to repay with interest within a reasonable time, by holding a potlatch of their own, would only compound their own humiliation and their host's glory.

A more recent viewpoint emphasizes the economic role of the potlatch in redistributing resources. It speculates that the pre-contact potlatch did not place as much importance on repayment with interest, which could be economically ruinous to those obliged to pay; and that the institution sometimes enabled a food-deficient group to survive a period of scarcity by offering blankets or other durable goods in exchange for food. In this light the potlatch may have been a helpful adaptation instead of the exhibition of waste and destruction reported by 19th century observers.[7] These extreme tendencies, in fact, point to the distorting influence of outside civilization which broke up the tight social structure, changed resource distribution patterns, and intensified "megalomanic" traits such as conspicuous consumption, subjugation of rivals, and self-glorification.

The impact of a machine-based technology seems also to have had a withering effect, ultimately, on NWC art. The initial effect, strangely enough, was to stimulate the production of most art forms. Metal tools and commercial paints acquired in trade speeded the production of totem poles for over a century. But the incandescence was temporary. The great strength of NWC art sprang from its intimate ties to the social structure. When the structure breaks apart, the art is no longer meaningful, nor is it produced with conviction. The peoples of the Northwest Coast still survive, but in numbers sharply depleted by disease and often as wards of the government or as employees of the white man. Here and there individuals pursue the old art forms, but the overall cultural impetus is lacking.

Fortunately many specimens of NWC art, produced when the culture was still cohesive, have been preserved. Erna Gunther refers to their "strength and self-assertive vitality"——qualities which are found in much primitive art, but which she maintains have been combined by Northwest Coast peoples with a "marked sensitivity to nuances of form and the highest standards of craftsmanship."[8] Some of these traits may be seen in the examples which follow.

13

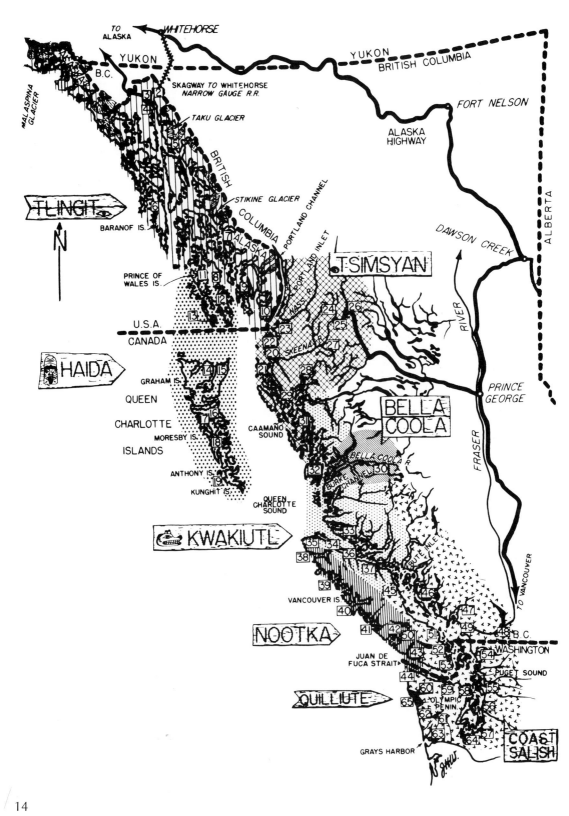

10. KEY TO MAP (Page 14) BY ETHNIC "NATION" AREAS

TLINGIT
1. Yakutat
2. Skagway
3. Haines and Port Chilkoot
4. Klukwan and Chilkat
5. Juneau, capital of Alaska
6. Sitka
7. Wrangell
8. Klawock
9. Ketchikan and Saxman
10. Cape Fox and Tongas
    (by 1900 the Kaigani-Haida of
    Prince of Wales Island claimed
    these old townsites)

HAIDA
11. Tuxecan
12. Kasaan
13. Howkan and Long Island
14. Yan
15. Massett
16. Skidegate
17. Tsal
18. Skedans, Tanu, Tasu
19. Ninstints (on Anthony Island)

TSIMSHIAN (TSIMSYAN)
20. Prince Rupert
21. Gitrhahla
22. Port Simpson
23. Fort Simpson
24. Kitwancool
25. Kitwanga
26. Hazelton and Kispiox
27. Kitsemkaelem
28. Kitimat
29. Hartley

BELLA COOLA
30. Bella Coola and Talio

KWAKIUTL
31. Princess Royal Island
32. Bellabella
33. Blunden Harbour
34. Fort Rupert
35. Koskimo
36. Alert Bay
37. Kelsey Bay

NOOTKA
38. Quatsino
39. Kyuquot
40. Nootka Sound and Nootka
41. Clayoquot Sound
42. Barkeley Sound, Sproat Lake, Alberni
43. Nitinat and Clo-oose
44. Cape Flattery, Makah, Neah Bay

COAST SALISH
45. Campbell River
46. Powell River
47. Squamish
48. Harrison Hot Springs and Chilliwack
49. Vancouver
50. Port Alberni
51. Nanaimo
52. Cowichan Lake and Duncan
53. Victoria (Songhees), capital of
    British Columbia
54. Bellingham
55. Tullalip and Everett
56. Seattle
57. Tacoma and Puyallup
58. Chimaukum, Sequim, Port
    Townsend
59. Port Angeles
60. Forks
61. Lake Quinault and Amanda
    Park
62. Queets
63. Hoquiam and Aberdeen
64. Olympia, capital of Washington

QUILLIUTE
65. La Push and Hoh

11. KEY TO CHILCAT BLANKET SPACE FILLERS

1. Man's head
2. Man's face, half.
3. Salmon-trout's head
4. Side of nose
5. Eyebrow
6. Eye
7. Black eye
8. Double eye or/"head of the salmon trout"
9. Goggles

10. Mouth
11. Cheek or jaw
12. Nostril
13. Ear
14. Hand, paw or foot
15. One in another
16. Side-holes
17. Holes, gambling-stick ends, or raindrops
18. Woman's hair ornament
19. Slit
20. Wing-feathers of red-winged flicker.

Each of these design units has a kind of completeness in itself, which might seem a detriment to the work as a whole, "but in practice . . . the parts are so interlocked and further united by the formal qualities they share, that the object invariably has a satisfying completeness about it."[1]

Erna Gunther

Raven   Bear

eyes

nostrils

"man's head"
 motif
containing
forehead lozenge
and
diamond teeth

claws

12.   Bear and [Ravens or Two Bear Cubs]. Chilcat blanket (copy).
       Chilcat, subtribe of Tlingit, NWC. Klukwan, Alaska, 19th century.
       Goat hair, cedar bark (original has top trimmed with sea otter and cedar bark fringe), 157 cm., AIAI.

Certainly this Chilcat blanket (Fig. 12) has an overall goggle-eye theme! The large
eyes just above center belong to a bear; below them can be recognized its jaws, nostrils,
and claws. The bear, the main design feature, seems engulfed in an array of elements
which are highly stylized and difficult to identify. The Chilcat blanket, in fact, is probably
the most abstract and least easily understood of all NWC art forms. Fig. 11 offers a key
to these abstract features. Where the bear's back and underside should be, for example,
are found several square "man's heads"* — a row of three above the bear's eyes, and one
beneath the nose.** These are SPACE FILLER devices which decorate what would other-
wise be blank areas in the design. But the space filling is not just mechanical. It seems to
arise from a tension "between the image and the area it fills," writes Erna Gunther, "so
that the resulting solution becomes a living balance between these opposing forces."
Circles are squared off, and each separate part seems compressed and tugged as though by
a magnetic force "exerted by the shape of the work as a whole."[2]

The urge to fill in space, frequently found in primitive art, is called "horror vacui,"
literally a horror or distaste of vacant, unadorned space. (Perhaps the half-conscious habit
of doodling reflects a similar tendency today.) To put it more positively, the artist may
simply have had a lively urge to activate the "dead" space with vivid representations and
meanings, to stretch every oval and curve to fit the overall design.

---

*   The interconnection between human and animal elements suggests the intimate bond between man and
       nature indicated by legends such as the Chilcat blanket legend, page 19.

**   In NWC art the square "man's head" design occurs only in the Chilcat blanket. A similar square head,
       however, is found in Peruvian Ocucaje textiles (600 B.C.); Bolivian Tiahuanacan idol (Fig. 94); in a gold
       breast plate from Coclé Province, Panama; in Shoshonean baskets from California; and in a bronze tiger
       (Chou Dynasty, China.) Each of these works has a jagged, bared, "N" teeth design.

main field   lateral field

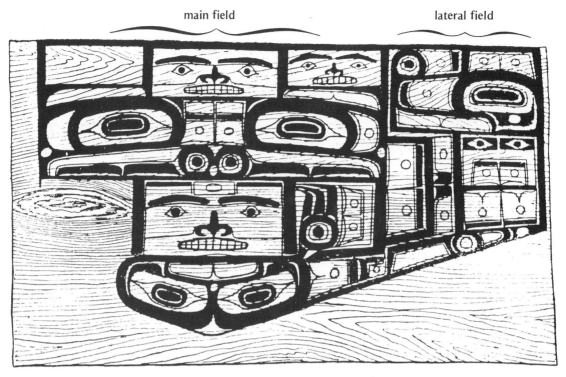

13.   Pattern board for Chilcat blanket.
The pattern after which a Chilcat blanket is woven is first painted on a board by a male artist. Since the blanket is symmetrical, only one of the two lateral sides is represented in the pattern.

14. The Chilcat woman weaving the blanket is using a "twining" process similar to that employed in making baskets—almost a unique method in this hemisphere. The sticks are for support; they are not part of the loom. Transforming the pattern into a blanket of yarn of shredded cedar bark, goat and dog's wool (white) takes a year of solid work. The colors and dyes for wool are much the same as for paint, except that urine is used to set the dye.

(Like their Northwest Coast counterparts, weavers of Maori flax cloaks used a "finger weaving" technique, adapted from basket making, along the garment's border.)

The Chilcat blanket: a legend from Tsimshian tradition

In the early days animals and human beings were close to one another; animals were regarded as just belonging to separate tribes, and their coats of fur could be removed at will, revealing their human form. Many traditions come from the brotherhood between animals and men. From these legends are derived the animal emblems of the families, seen in house posts and other NWC wood carvings.*

One day a chief's daughter went out with other women to gather wild celery — the first harbinger of spring and a relief from the winter diet of dried salmon and oil. In the forest she was embraced by a handsome youth, who persuaded her to follow him to his village to become his wife. She arrived, only to learn that he was of the Bear tribe.

She escaped, reached the shore, and was rescued by a fisherman, but only after promising to become his wife. Once afloat, the fisherman revealed himself as the benevolent sea spirit Gonaquadet, and together they descended to his great rock house at sea-bottom.

The chief's daughter became greatly attached to her gentle husband. But when she bore him a human son, Gonaquadet allowed her to return to earth so that the boy could be trained by his maternal uncle (to conform to the matrilineal system) — on the condition that she weave him a ceremonial robe to commemorate their meeting and courtship. This she faithfully did, and brought it to him when the son reached manhood. This was the origin of the Chilcat blanket.[3]

---

*   The ability of animals to take the form of other animals or of humans is reflected in much NWC art, including the blanket in Fig. 12, in which the creatures seem to interlink with one another.

ears

15. *T'ao t'ieh* (monster mask design).
     "Ting" (ceremonial food container).
     Shang Dynasty, China, 16th—11th century B.C.
     Bronze, 9¼".

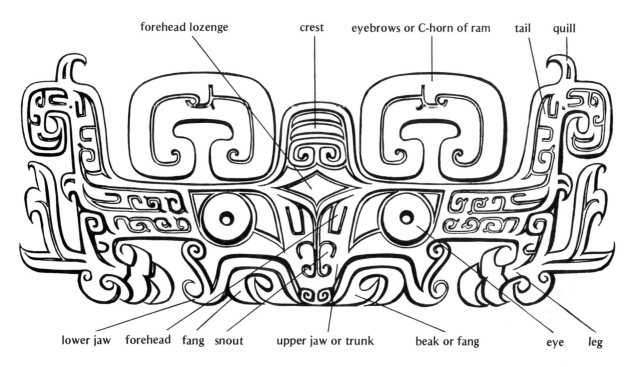

forehead lozenge   crest   eyebrows or C-horn of ram   tail   quill

lower jaw   forehead   fang   snout   upper jaw or trunk   beak or fang   eye   leg

16.   Diagram of *T'ao T'ieh* on *Ting*.
(Monster mask on ceremonial food container.)

As in the Chilcat blanket, the design elements of this Chinese bronze ceremonial container *("Ting")** have been deliberately adapted and rearranged, filling in the space symmetrically and leaving almost no undecorated area. The two sides facing the viewer contain a mask representing a *t'ao t'ieh*, interpreted as a dragon, a crocodile, a noxious spirit of hills and wastes, or a combination of many animals in one form. Diagram 16 identifies the stylized features. The head can be seen simultaneously as a full face or two meeting profiles.** Rhythmically filling in the area around the mask is a design of repeated squared spirals. The V-shaped motif on the legs may depict either knife blades, a sacrificial sign; or the cicada, symbol of regeneration. Note how the C-horn is enlarged to fit the space between crest and tail, and how the claw-leg fills in under the body.

In addition to its religious function, the *"Ting"* was an indicator of social status. Marks were cast on a *"Ting"* to denote persons or clans who owned it. Inscriptions designate use in sacrifice to an ancestor. Perceval Yetts writes, "The impulse [to possess a *"Ting"*] seems almost invariably to have been self-glorification, even when show is made of solacing ancestors or of enhancing the family prestige."[4]

---

*   In addition to its literal meaning of sacrificial vessel or caldron, *"Ting"* is used to mean imperial or political power, or empire.

**   For a similar instance in NWC art, see Fig. 25.

17.   Ainu, Japan.
      *The man wears on his head a headring made
      from elm-fibre, on which is fastened a totem-
      sign carved from soft wood—of a bear or fox.*

18.   **Chief Shakes with Killer Whale Staff of Office.**
      Tlingit, Northwest Coast.
      *Copy of painting, (original by W. Langdon Kihn,
          1943) by Jaques L. Conder 1962.*
      Pastel, 19" x 25". AIAI.
      The Chilcat blanket is worn like a cape by the
chief of the clan for ceremonies such as the potlatch.
Movement in dancing is emphasized by its long fringe.
      The Chilcats are the only tribe among the North-
west Coast known for this style of blanket weaving.

19.   **Ainu Robe**
      Piratori, Japan.
      Appliqué.
      Similar to the Chilcat cape-blanket, this *Ainu*
(aboriginal tribe of Hokkaido, Japan) robe is ceremonial and is worn with the clan headpiece. The lively curved
designs are broken into similar light and dark patterns.
Usually, an abstract design is derived from many re-
workings of a realistic representation; and, in this case,
one can almost "see" an animal from which this
abstract motif may have been derived.

Quetzal feathered head-dress, enlarged to fill space, show status

jade earplugs of nobleman

very heavy necklace, perhaps symbolizing the firegod

Pictograph interpretation: →
dog with tongue out emerging from earth monster's jaw; three teeth below; claw and "spare" foot may symbolize a path.[5]

20.   Zapotec Culture Hero, named "8 Dog."
      Relief, carved slab (reproduction).
      Monte Alban III, Mexico, 700 A.D.
      Stone, 10" x 4½" AIAI.

This Zapotec culture hero is skillfully designed to enliven all available space. The large head and headdress, as in most cultures, emphasizes important status. "Someone who is someone is depicted as **more** of someone," especially by adding a symbol of achieved status. (In some Northwest Coast tribes tall hats perform a similar function—see Fig. 88.)

In Zapotec culture each child at birth is given a guardian spirit or *nagual* (Zapotec *nahualli,* to know). The spirit is represented by an animal influencing his life and determining his death. The headdress in this piece probably identifies the owner's *nagual,* which is disguised to all but the initiated.[6] Added to this headdress, like most, are the beautiful blue-green iridescent feathers of the quetzalbird, symbolic of life.

The dog in the earth monster's head is a pictograph, perhaps telling the name of the hero and a date or dayname related to a festival when his memory was celebrated. It resembles Mayan glyphs (see Fig. 91). It is interesting also to compare the whole hero figure to figures on the Great Idol of Tiahuanaco, Fig. 92.

Note that the open mouth
is a hole on a spindle whorl.

Meeting otter profiles simultaneously become
frontal face as in Ts'un figure, Fig. 32.

Drawing of Fig. 21.

claw feet

corn cob
headdress

toad qualities
on head

21.   Figure and two otters.
        Spindle whorl.
        Salish, 19th C.
        Northwest Coast.
        Wood, 8½".

eagle claws
on hands
and feet

22.   Aztec Earth-Toad God, Tlaltecuhtli.
        Codex Barbonicus, 1500 A.D.

        This earth god devours men and the sun,
and has a counterpart, the earth mother, who
remits sins and is in charge of childbirth. For
more discussion of Tlaltecuhtli, see Fig. 58.

Depicting a three-dimensional object on a flat or semi-flat surface is a basic problem
in design. One solution is to show both sides of the figure frontally, producing a symmetrical pattern often called "bilateral split." A bilaterally split object appears "splayed"
or spread out flat like the "bear" in a bear rug. In this respect, the next several items,
(Fig. 21 through Fig. 34), offer an intriguing resemblance. Most of the figures illustrated,
from widely separated cultures around the Pacific Basin, are depicted sitting on their
haunches (M-shape for lower part of body) with their arms and knees raised (W-shape for
upper part). The out-thrust arms generally seem to relate to the power of a supernatural
female being to protect her offspring and descendants.

23. **Splayed figure.**
Pottery Bowl.
Mimbres culture, 900 A.D.
Swart's Ruin, Arizona

knee and elbow
joint marks

24. **Body of a Figure.**
Funeral pot.
Yang Shao, China, 7,000–6,000 B.C.
Red pottery, white, black, red paint.
Neck opening is head.
Red lines represent blood stream.

25

Quetzal or corncob headdress

snake "hands" variation of
crocodile god.

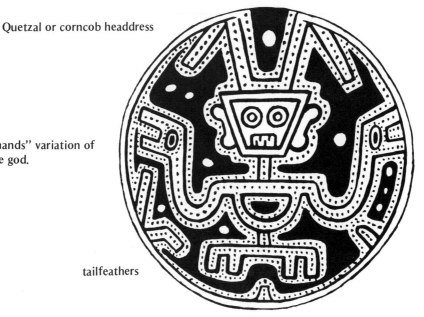

tailfeathers

25.   Figure with snake and bird appendages.
      Pottery dish.
      Nicoya, Costa Rica.

corncob headdress

earplugs

monkey-head appendages

26.   Figure with monkey appendages.
      Tapestry.
      Central Peruvian Coast.

webbed or claw feet

27. Diagram of jar design.
Coclé.
Province of Chiriqui, Panama.
Ceramic, 11¼" approx.

Compare the strong resemblance in facial style between this Coclé (Panama) figure and that of Fig. 30 from the Northwest Coast. Fig. 37, also from Coclé, shows the whole body clearly splayed.

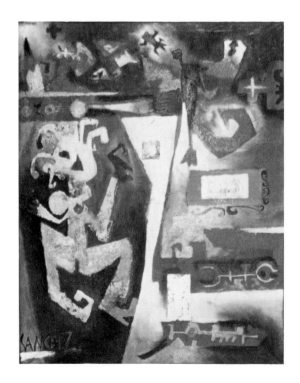

28. Painting.
A modern adaptation
of the split figure motif.
By Enrique Sanchez, Bogota, Columbia, 1950(?)
Casein. AIAI.

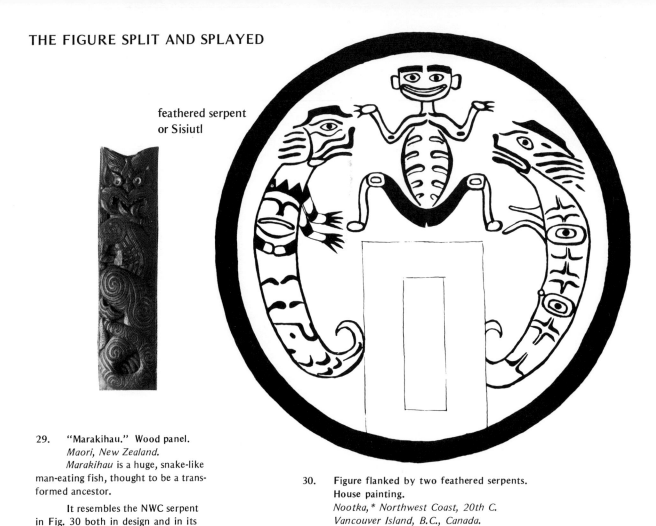

feathered serpent
or Sisiutl

29.   "Marakihau." Wood panel.
Maori, New Zealand.
Marakihau is a huge, snake-like man-eating fish, thought to be a transformed ancestor.

It resembles the NWC serpent in Fig. 30 both in design and in its ancestral depiction.

30.   Figure flanked by two feathered serpents. House painting.
Nootka, * *Northwest Coast, 20th C.*
Vancouver Island, B.C., Canada.
Wood, paint.

The design in Fig. 30 was painted around the door to the chief's dwelling. The splayed figure has large but human ears,* and is surrounded by two horned serpents ("Sisiutl" —see Fig. 35). Unless one has an established right, touching the Sisiutl or passing beneath him to get inside the house is considered a fatal act. But when the chief passes through the door, it is considered a re-enactment of his guardian animal transformation—the process by which he acquires, as does every male clan member, a personal animal totem from his direct ancestor at the time of his initiation into manhood.** The chief's manhood initiation also establishes his claim to "chiefhood."[1] (See also Fig. 57).

---

*   In the Northwest Coast the splayed figure is limited largely to the more southern tribes. In NWC art the ears will quickly tell you whether the figure is animal or human. Human ears appear to the side of the head; animal ears are on top.

**   See discussion of transformation on p. 72.

28

Shotkaman—Agwi

large bird, *gandju*

great snake, lizard or land nourished by the channel of water created by the lizard

phallic symbols of prankster, Betman Gambi, or yams

31. Splayed figure "Shotkaman-Agwi"; birds, snake or lizard. Ritual Object. *Eastern Iatmul, Sepik River, New Guinea. Wood, twine, paint, 16½".*

snake or lizard passing from woman to Betman Gambi (resurrection)

Compare the arrangement of the Nootka (NWC) figure (Fig. 30) flanked by two curving snakes, with that of the New Guinea figure (Fig. 31). The splayed figure from New Guinea represents Shotkaman-Agwi, an early female clan ancestor:*

> In legend the woman travelled up one of the tributaries of the Sepik River where she gave birth to the *gandju* bird** and at the same time to the great snake or lizard. The latter wriggled to the sea, gouging out the present sinuous course of the Sepik River.

Shotkaman-Agwi is flanked on top by two *gandju* birds and below by the male prankster, Betman-Gambi (note the phallic forms on either side). When he died, the woman's snake awakened life in him.[2]

Northwest Coast legend includes similar characters: the great Thunderbird (teacher of culture), his companion the water snake Sisiutl, and Raven, the prankster.

Like Shotkaman-Agwi, the Aztec earth god (Fig. 22) has an associated resurrecting quality. The Northwest Coast and Maori (Fig. 34) examples also have an implicit power of resurrection or rebirth.

---

* This splayed figure motif of New Guinea is often found on sacred houses and war shields. See p. 51 for a discussion of the guardian-birth aspects associated with this figure, which include the origin of clans, resurrection, and the warding off of hostile forces.

** The *gandju* is the totem of a local group in the middle Sepik region. See Trickster Raven legend, p. 77.

simultaneous image
forehead lozenge

tiger (symbol of earth)

32. Ts'un Figure and two tigers.
     Chou Dynasty.
     Anhwei Province, China.
     Bronze.
     There is speculation as to the meaning
of the tigers' position: Are they devouring
the human, or are they protecting him as a
totem animal or alter ego?

33. Splayed figure wearing double-headed
     serpent headpiece, flanked by cats.
     Stone lintel.
     Marka-Kunka, 100 B.C.—500 A.D.;
     Cajamarquilla, near Huaraz, Peru.

Cats may represent
images of the sun
and moon

Double-headed snake
is earth symbol

This Peruvian lintel was probably situated over a doorway to a building or tomb, or over the entrance way of a fortified town; any of these locations suggest a protective function, also indicated by the association of the splayed figure motif with headhunting.* The splayed figures from the Sepik River (New Guinea) and the Maori cultures (Fig. 29 and 34) are also closely linked with headhunting, and this motif is often seen on shields in these areas.   (The Haida tribe of the Northwest Coast also collected human heads as trophies.)

According to Douglas Newton, headhunting among people of the Sepik River of New Guinea enabled them to posses the life-force of the enemy and also to "transmute the victims into fertility-giving ancestors."**[3] The Maoris, too, believed that by rubbing captured heads against female genitalia, the heads were transmuted into ancestors of the group which captured them; the ritual also served to defile the victims.[4]

---

*   See trophy head on belt of Peruvian man, Fig. 74.

**   The soul is represented in Eskimo masks to ensure hunting success and fertility.

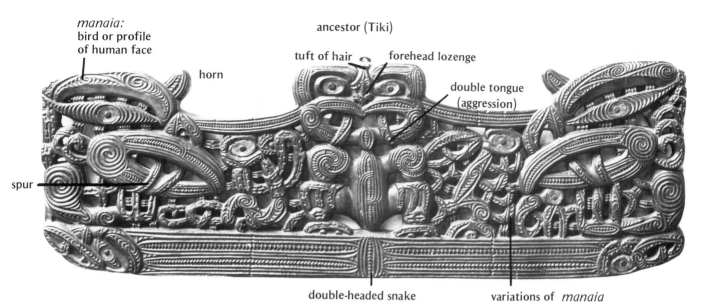

manaia:
bird or profile
of human face

ancestor (Tiki)

tuft of hair

forehead lozenge

horn

double tongue
(aggression)

spur

double-headed snake

variations of *manaia*

34.   Splayed figure, *Manaia* birds, with base of double-headed snake.
       House lintel.
       Maori, New Zealand, before 1867.
       Wood, (carved with stone tools), red paint, * *3' and 1.5'.*

The two-tongued goddess** in Fig. 34 is flanked by "bird-men" on the right and left, all atop a double-headed snake. In Maori belief an important *female* function is to protect the men and *mana* (power and prestige) of her clan, and to repel or destroy intruders. A favorite Maori legend recounts how the trickster-hero Maui, who aggressively sought dispensations which were denied him, was trapped and killed by the goddess of death.†

Illustrated objects from the Northwest Coast (Fig. 30), China (Fig. 32) and Peru (Fig. 33) are similar to this Maori lintel in Fig. 34. All depict a splayed female figure; all (except Fig. 32) were once situated above doorways; and all had a function of counter-aggression.

Among all these splayed figures two characteristics have become apparent. First, the association of the figure with two flanking animal forms, usually reptile and/or bird; second, the figure's appendages, especially claw-feet (perhaps those of a bird or reptile). These associations suggest a dualism (two creatures or natures in one) which provides fascinating clues as to the thought-content which underlies these works. Dualism can be seen in many of the works to follow, especially those in the next section.

---

*   Its red color represents the power of the gods, *mana,* and was made by mixing red clay and shark liver oil.

**   In numerous other Maori renditions a central figure flanked by two bird creatures is clearly female.

†   The Polynesian concept of birds as intermediaries with the dead strengthens the suggestion of the "death goddess" role. See discussion of *manaia* and *mana,* p. 61.

31

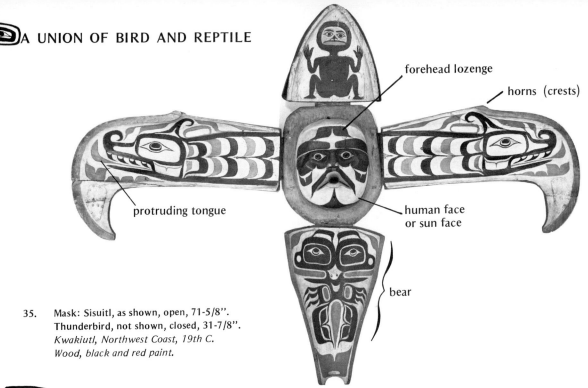

forehead lozenge

horns (crests)

protruding tongue

human face
or sun face

bear

35. Mask: Sisiutl, as shown, open, 71-5/8".
     Thunderbird, not shown, closed, 31-7/8".
     Kwakiutl, Northwest Coast, 19th C.
     Wood, black and red paint.

Thunderbird, in Northwest Coast mythology, can dispatch deadly strokes of lightning. But Northwest Coast peoples from the Chinook in the south to the Tlingit in the north believe that Thunderbird "gets his power from a fish which he seizes and hides in his feathers."[1] When Thunderbird "darts one of the fish down with great velocity," lightning flashes from Thunderbird's serpent-like tongue.[2] Lightning, in fact, was identified with Sisiutl, a two-headed serpent and a prominent figure in NWC legends. Sisiutl was used by Thunderbird to hunt whales.[3] This is one of many legends showing the close "transformation" association of Thunderbird and Sisiutl.

When this Thunderbird mask (Fig. 35) is spread out, as shown, Sisiutl is depicted by the two horizontal arms. The central man-like face indicates Sisiutl's power to assume human form. When the wearer of the mask jerks on hidden strings the wings fold together, enclosing all these features inside, and the outside surface suddenly "becomes" a Thunderbird.[4] (A Thunderbird-Sisiutl mask in *both* open and closed positions is shown in Fig. 84).*

The legend attributed to the mask (Fig. 35) is this:

> A man tried, but without success, to find the Sisiutl for his magical treasure, and died. His tribe made him a false grave with the sun painted on it. However, because he actually had found the magical treasure, Sisiutl took him away to heaven. Four days later it thundered. The man had been changed by Sisiutl into the shape of a Thunderbird and came down to the beach. He took off his mask representing his treasures (Shaman's powers) and showed the people its two faces.**[5]

---

*   Also see separate sections on Thunderbird, and double-headed serpents.

**   Thunderbird also occurs in Eskimo legend. One legend recounts a Thunderbird (not illustrated) who preyed on whales and whose wingspread exceeded the whale's length. Because Thunderbird ate people as well, he was finally killed by a hunter avenging his wife's death.[6]

Quetzal headdress of the
celestial rain God-bird Tlaloc

jaguar

goggle eyes of Firegod
Xiutecuhtli

earplugs

forked serpent's tongue

serpent's mouth

possible day counts?

36. Tlaloc, the plumed serpent.
Earthenware bowl with fresco decoration.
Teotihuacan culture, Mexico, 400 B.C.–800 A.D.
Clay with paint on plaster layer, white, yellow,
sienna and black, 3" or 9.7 cm.

This rain god of Teotihuacan, Tlaloc, is in charge of
a special heaven for warriors and their protector. Half-
way down the bowl beneath the bird headdress, we see a
row of four double circles. The inside two show the fire
god's slit eyes peering out of "goggles"; the outside two
are his high-ranking "ear plugs"! The ear plugs may come
in handy, too, when Tlaloc displays his power.

The fresco decoration on the bowl is utterly un-
typical of potters' techniques, and is so fragile that few
examples have survived, but the effect is gorgeous. See
also the Aztec splayed eagle-toad, Fig. 58.

Because the type of mask shown in Fig. 35 depicts dual or multiple identity through
the abrupt emergence of one form out of another, it is called a "transformation mask."*
It was used, especially by the Kwakiutl, to bring about a dramatic interchange between
two different beings. The duality of Thunderbird and Sisiutl, for instance, suggests the
joining of two opposites: Thunderbird representing the upper, heavenly world, and Sisiutl,
the earthly.

Note the curved crest on each of Sisiutl's heads. (Fig. 35). It is curious how frequently among the art of certain Pacific Basin cultures the reptile is "crested," or possibly
plumed (see Fig. 36, Teotihuacan culture, Mexico). The occurrence of this bird-like feature
atop a reptile points again to a synthesis of contrasting elements, a union of upper and
lower worlds.

Other serpent-bird combinations can be seen in the Peruvian winged man with snake-
eye decorations (Fig. 74); in a winged creature with a snout and a spiral tail (Fig. 92 —
pictograph on Bolivian goddess); in the snake intertwining with a bird (Fig. 83, from New
Ireland); and in the Toltec plumed serpent (Fig. 43).

---

*   More about transformation masks p. 72.

open jaws point upward
suggestive of an earth
monster swallowing the sun

crocodile foot
and bird's tail

crest

black vulture

37. Crocodile-bird god with human body.
     Gold repoussé disk.
     8½"
     Coclé, Panama. 800—1200 A.D.

38.   Quetzalcoatl, The Plumed Serpent or the planet Venus.
       Stone tablet 61 cm.
       Toltec, Mexico, Early Post-classic, 700 A.D.

The Toltec Quetzal (bird)—coatl (serpent) represents wisdom, creation and life. The two-headed god saved man from four disasters, wind, fire, water and tigers, recreating man each time.

39.   *T'ao T'ieh* (monster mask).
       "Ting" (ceremonial container).
       Shang Dynasty, China, 16th century, B.C.
       Bronze, 9¼"

Reptile elements are combined with bird features such as the beak, quills, and crest. The diagram was previously shown and discussed, Fig. 16. Also see the Shang Bird-man-crocodile on a drum, Fig. 69.

40. Two-headed sea monster with shaman.
Pendant.
Northwest Coast.
Ivory and Haliotis shell inlay.

A favorite avocation of art historians is to account for striking resemblances among cultural objects widely separated in time or location. A two-headed snake form with a figure or face between the two snakes is common among Northwest Coast carvings, and is called Sisiutl by the Kwakiutl tribe. But a similar combination also appears in art objects from China, Mexico, Panama and Peru, all illustrated in this section. It is suggested that the double-headed serpent is a traditional early Asiatic sculptural motif which spread (or "diffused") through the Pacific Basin. If this theory is valid, and the similarities among the examples in this section can be explained by assuming cultural contact, there appears to have been remarkably little alteration of the original basic design, despite the huge gap in time and the distances these cultural elements had to travel. From this perspective, some NWC carvings executed within the last 150 years have preserved the ancient origin of their design amazingly well.[1]

Sisiutl (portrayed as a two-headed sea monster in Fig. 40) was a versatile being who could change himself into human form at will, as indicated by the human figure, or shaman, in the middle. He had the power to retrieve souls by swallowing (compare the story of Jonah and the whale), and to perform enormous supernatural feats. (See legends and discussion of Thunderbird and Sisiutl, p. 32).

41.   Sisiutl.
       Soul Catcher.
       Tsimshian, NWC.
       Niska tribe at Kitikshan, Lower Nass River.
       Bone, Haliotis shell inlay, 7½".

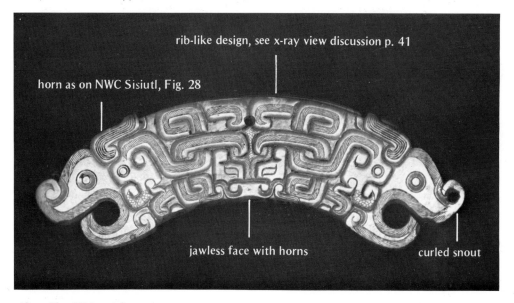

rib-like design, see x-ray view discussion p. 41

horn as on NWC Sisiutl, Fig. 28

jawless face with horns

curled snout

42.   *T'ao-T'ieh* and face.
       Jade pendant ornament 4½".
       Eastern Chou, 771–600 B.C.
       C'hu area, China.

Some Chou motifs of the *T'ao-T'ieh* show it unsuccessfully swallowing a man, symbolizing retribution.* **

---

*   An Eskimo horned crocodile, "Polraiyuk," swallows people, but is not double-headed. It is shown with circles at intervals, each containing a different part of a man. There is also a double-headed snake (Fig. 54), though it does not include a human head.[2]

**   A Maori snake-fish (Fig. 29) represents a transformed ancestor who swallows men and canoes through his tongue.

Quetzalcoatl, who represented life to the Toltecs (Fig. 38), has a similar meaning in this Zapotec object (Fig. 43). It is shown in combination with the batgod, symbol of death, and the jaguar.

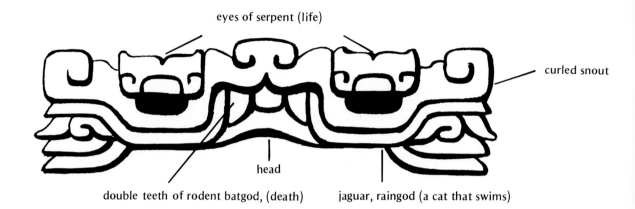

eyes of serpent (life)

curled snout

head

double teeth of rodent batgod, (death)

jaguar, raingod (a cat that swims)

43. Jaguar batgod.
    Clay urn.
    Zapotec, Oaxaca, Mexico; 1–800 A.D.

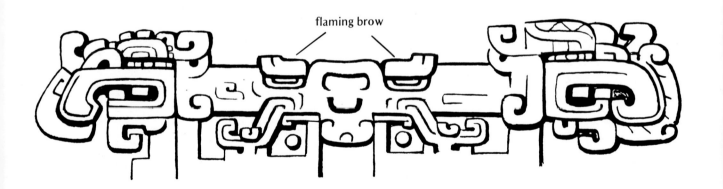

flaming brow

44. Fire-Raingod, Dual life-death design over tomb entrance.
    Stone stele.
    El Meson, Veracruz, Mexico.
    Mayan culture, 900 A.D.

45. Crocodile god.
    Ceramic jar.
    Coclé, 1450's.
    Grave 5, Sitio Conté, Panama.
    Late polychrome, fine-line style, 13¾".

crest   curved snout

crest

46. Diagram of crocodile god jar.
    Coclé, Panama.

This diagram shows both frontal and profile views of a crocodile. The belt streamer goes from the "frontal" eye to the "profile" eye.

figure holds arrow-shaped knife, has mouth mask, head ornament

protruding tongue of "goatsucker," mythological being with monkey feet

47. Double-headed snake and Goatsucker.   This double-headed snake has cat faces, human arms, and many head appendages.
Altar cloth (detail).
Paracas, Peru, 1500 B.C.–500 A.D.
Tan cotton with red alpaca double-faced embroidery, 1.090 m. x .375 m.

In Nazca art, which followed Paracas art, a similar double-headed serpent motif was worshipped as a local god, symbolizing a mythical clan ancestor.[3]

The two-headed snake as an architectural decorative motif in gates and doors is explored by Ralph Coe. His illustrations show the motif displayed in widely different settings: as a Sisiutl (NWC, Kwakiutl tribe) across a house front doorway; as a Chinese (pre-Han, 520 A.D.) two-headed dragon-beam holding a gong; as a Chinese two-headed snake over a niche containing Buddha;* as an Indian snake ("Makara") on the gates of Sanchi-stupa; and as a horizontal element, in a more abstract form, of a Japanese Torii gate, the snouts of the snake's heads conforming to the upturned ends of the gate.**[4]

---

* The Northwest Coast Sisiutl and the Chinese two-headed snake both have a protruding tongue.

** See "House Totem Posts," p. 88 (asterisked footnote) for a discussion of the double-headed serpent as used in sacred houses.

48.   Paracas costume showing double-headed serpent motif.
      Peru, 1500 B.C.—500 A.D.

In this robe, as in many Peruvian textiles, units are made in pieces and sewn or woven together, a method approximating the NWC Chilcat blanket technique.[5]

49.   Bear flanked by two profile animals. tongue — instrument of power, voraciousness
      Coffin front on a mortuary pole.
      Haida, NWC.
      Wood and paint.

To "stick out one's tongue" at someone is a mocking sign, a harmless grade-school prank. How amusing, and strange, to find this half-forgotten gesture brought to life—and staring down at one from massive Northwest Coast totem poles, most often as part of a bear. A bit of investigation reveals the "protruding tongue" occurring in the art forms of other cultures around the Pacific Basin. Scholars favoring cultural diffusion as the explanation for the astonishing range of this feature—from Alaska to New Zealand— speculate that it may have originated in ancient China, then spread in several directions (see Chart, Fig. 7). Numerous examples of the protruding tongue motif survive from the Chou Dynasty. One scholar, after an extensive comparison of the protruding tongue in NWC and Maori art, concluded that the significance was not just that the "tongue" occurs in both traditions, but that it occurs in both cases **in the same complex variations.** This detailed resemblance, he felt, was difficult to account for unless some cultural contact had taken place.[1] No one, though, claims to know the exact historical process through which this cultural borrowing occurred over such vast distances.

The protruding tongue was undoubtedly used with more serious intent by native artists than its aura of mischief might first suggest. In most Pacific Basin cultures it seems to have denoted supernatural power. Northwest Coast peoples often considered the long tongue a sign of special powers. Among the Tsimshian and Northern Haida, one who tore out the tongue of an otter was entitled to "call upon the creatures of the unseen world to do his bidding."[2] The appearance of the protruding tongue on carvings of bears, wolves, and sea animals signifies the underlying presence of Sisiutl, an important and somewhat sinister being who had the power to assume many roles.*   (See Fig. 32.) Thus prominently displayed, the tongue was a clear indication of supernatural powers. Among the Maori it was also a sign of power, and sticking out the tongue was thought to give a man's face a ferocious expression during ritual dances[3] —a sign of the prowess and aggressiveness expected of a warrior. (See Fig. 51.)

---

*   See section on Two-headed Serpent for a discussion of Sisiutl, p. 36.

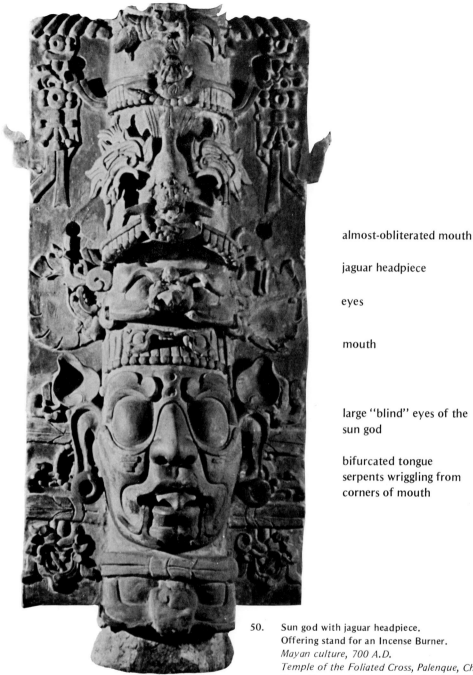

almost-obliterated mouth

jaguar headpiece

eyes

mouth

large "blind" eyes of the
sun god

bifurcated tongue
serpents wriggling from
corners of mouth

50. Sun god with jaguar headpiece.
     Offering stand for an Incense Burner.
     Mayan culture, 700 A.D.
     Temple of the Foliated Cross, Palenque, Chiapas, Mexico.
     Terra Cotta, painted turquoise (sacrificial color), red,
         yellow, and white, 41¼".

On either side of the Mayan sungod's tongue (Fig. 50) is a wriggling snake. The god combines the qualities of warrior, eagle and jaguar. He wears a jaguar headpiece and is nourished by human blood. Earth becomes dark as the warrior sun god passes through the underworld at night, emerging to chase away the stars in the morning.

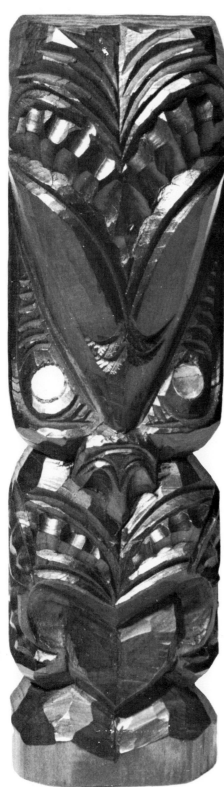

protruding
tongue

51.   Carved head representing an ancestor.
Maori, New Zealand, 1974.
Wood and abalone shell, AIAI.
       Along with its expressions of defiance,
supernatural power, and protective-aggressive
power, the out-thrust tongue carries with it a
phallic implication.

eyebrows drawn out
to fill in the corners
of the rectangular shape

In Maori art, the protruding tongue served the additional purpose of warding off evil by means of its power to harm. The more grotesque and the less naturalistic a figure was, for example, the greater its aggressive, semi-divine power. Another indication of this "idolized" aggression is the figure's eyes (see Fig. 51). A legend tells how the Maori carvings acquired these large staring eyes:

> Rongo, an ancient Maori artist, supposedly learned his knowledge of carving and carved designs from a house of the celestial realm. When he constructed his own house one day he used Koururu, the personified form of the owl *(ruru)*, as a sacred offering which he buried beneath the rear wall. From that day many Maori carvings were constructed with the burning eyes of the owl; they are the eyes of Koururu.*4

Often at night, when the Maori people would gather by firelight or moonlight to hear tales of the past and affairs of the day, the shell-inlaid eyes of the carvings were reflected in the light accentuating their ancestors' fierce aspect. The defiant quality which made the warrior especially esteemed was also displayed in these figures, not only by the glaring eyes, but by the protruding tongue as well.

---

*   The owl is a Maori omen bird and carrier of spirits.

44

protruding tongue
to repel enemies
and hostile spirits

52.   Ancestor's face shield.
       Sepik River Valley, New Guinea, early 20th C.
       Wood, white earth, red clay, black, 5'5".

       Even today, as traditionally, all members of
some New Guinea communities are sculptors. Though
not all are equally talented, many are capable of producing art objects of museum quality.

The protruding tongue (previous section) hints at interior forces externalized. Now we see a visual approach, shared by many cultures, which seems to penetrate the body anatomically. In Figures 53—56 the inner structure of the body is illuminated, and the outer surface decorated, by a kind of x-ray vision. The side sections of the Tlingit (NWC) ceremonial robe (Fig. 53) clearly depict the spinal column, teeth and ribs of the animal.* A rib pattern can also be detected in the Eskimo drawing (Fig. 54) of a seal and two-headed serpent, in the New Guinea panel (Fig. 56), where the ribs form a design repeated as a space filler between figures, and in the Maori carving (Fig. 55).** In Fig. 54 an Eskimo artist's unique vision allows us to see through to an animal's bladder and other internal features. Since the bladder was considered the seat of an animal's soul, this inward penetration seems not only anatomical but metaphysical.

The next section, "Joint Marks," presents a special aspect of the inner view concept.

---

* The Ainu (aborigines of Japan) similarly depict the spinal column, considering it the "seat of vitality." It is found on a figurine from Itarogi Prefecture (not illustrated).

** Picasso's paintings, strongly influenced by primitive art, frequently have a quality of interior penetration. In his "Young Woman with a Looking-glass" (1932) the rib lines of his subject are prominently depicted.

46

53. Chief's Ceremonial Robe.
Tlingit, NWC, 19th C.
Cape Fox, Alaska.
Caribou skin, bear claws, painted red and black, 45" x 60"

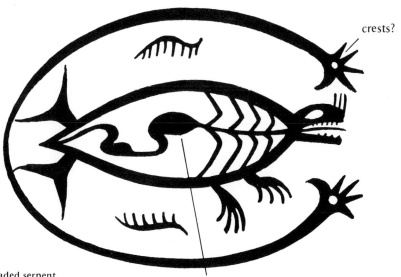

crests?

bladder representing seal's soul

54. Seal and two-headed serpent.
Tray
Eskimo, 19th C.
Wood.

top knot of hair

slanting, staring owl eyes, see Fig. 66

upturned three-claw hands

rib design

web feet

55.   Ancestor god.
      House lintel.
      Maori culture, New Zealand.
      Wood.
      Early Maori art was carved by a
      craftsman-priest. Around 1769 their
      special religious status began to decline
      as traditional values were influenced by
      European ways. With new tools art be-
      came more decorative and less sculptural.

56. Male and female ancestor-figures and heads of wattled or crested birds. Sheath or panel for cult building. *Keram River, Lower Sepik, New Guinea. Sago palm spathe, bamboo, paint.* 3'4-1/8" x 5' 3-3/4".

Keram River art motifs are governed by tradition and ownership privileges which can be sold.

ribs and joint-marks

49

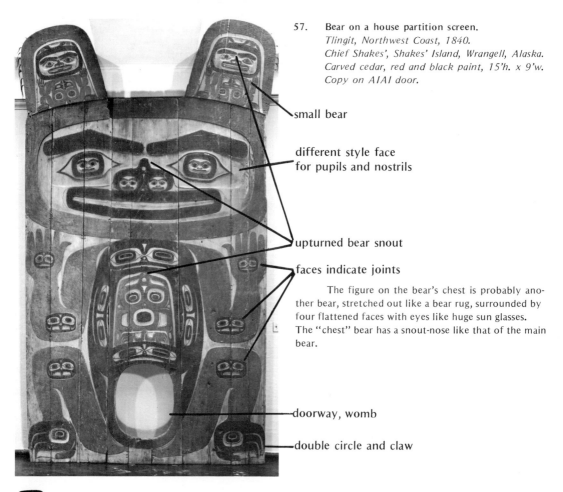

57. Bear on a house partition screen.
Tlingit, Northwest Coast, 1840.
Chief Shakes', Shakes' Island, Wrangell, Alaska.
Carved cedar, red and black paint, 15'h. x 9'w.
Copy on AIAI door.

small bear

different style face
for pupils and nostrils

upturned bear snout

faces indicate joints

The figure on the bear's chest is probably another bear, stretched out like a bear rug, surrounded by four flattened faces with eyes like huge sun glasses. The "chest" bear has a snout-nose like that of the main bear.

doorway, womb

double circle and claw

Joint marks can be considered as a special manifestation of the "x-ray" concept. In the following examples, from many cultures, the joint connections of the wrist, elbow, knee or shoulder have been dramatized by some kind of circular mark.

In the Tlingit (NWC) bear (Fig. 57) the markings appear as tiny faces. On other Northwest Coast objects such as the owl (Fig. 66) "eyes" are employed as joint marks. Two theories have been suggested to explain this occurrence. One is that the outer circle represents the socket and the inner circle the ball; the second is that because all joints are movable they are presented as having eyes wherewith to govern their motion. The Aztecs marked each joint with a double-circle eye on an eagle claw. (Fig. 58). Double circles which indicate not only joint marks but also real eyes appear in various cultures of Alaska (Fig. 65), New Guinea (Fig. 62), and the Northwest Coast (Fig. 64).*

---

* Also see the "joint marks" on the Chinese splayed figures (Figs. 24 and 69).

A Tlingit (NWC) chief had to pass through the bear's "abdominal mouth" (Figs. 57 and 30) in order to get to his living quarters.* With this act, symbolizing disappearance and rebirth, the chief and his family continually re-established their hereditary claims with the supernatural.** An outsider or non-clan member risked being "devoured" if he entered the chief's area through this "transformational" opening.

The Maoris of New Zealand entered their villages through a hole at least four feet high in a tall wooden gateway carved with ancestor images.[1] As in the Northwest Coast, disaster could befall a Maori commoner who intruded upon his chief or the chief's possessions.†

The "abdominal mouth" in Fig. 57, clearly analogous to the female sex organ, is supposed to symbolize not only rebirth but also guardian protection of offspring;[2] in this case, the chief is the sacred progeny protected by the female guardian ancestor. This idea relates to the anatomical-visual approach discussed on page 42, and specifically to the statement that "this inward [visual] penetration seems not only anatomical but metaphysical."

---

* This well-known Tlingit bear screen from Chief Shakes' house was copied from an earlier version now located at the Washington State Museum. The screen had been removed before the house was destroyed in 1937. A photo of the reconstructed house appears in Fig. 106, and a copy of the screen may be seen on a door at the AIAI.

** See discussions on "guardian animal," pp. 11 and 23.

† See the splayed figures, pp. 21—34. The use of a *facial* mouth as a doorway is common to cultures from the Northwest Coast, Meso-America (Aztec, Maya, Mixtec), and Southeast Asia (Java, Bali, Cambodia); and possibly to ancient China.[3]

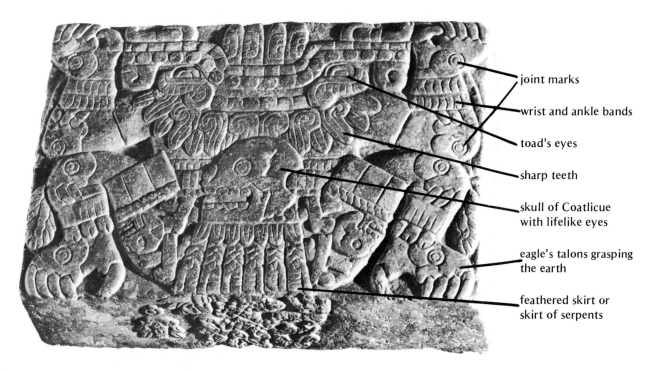

joint marks

wrist and ankle bands

toad's eyes

sharp teeth

skull of Coatlicue
with lifelike eyes

eagle's talons grasping
the earth

feathered skirt or
skirt of serpents

58.   Earth monster, Tlaltecuhtli.
       Stone box bottom.
       Aztec culture, Texcoco(?), Mexico, 1470 A.D.
       Gray green mottled stone, 13-1/8" x 8-1/4" x 6".

Donut-shaped joint marks are clearly revealed by the splayed position of Tlaltecuhtli, Aztec toad-earth monster, which appears in Figs. 22 and 58. Prominently displayed in the center of the figure is a "skull god" * with sharp teeth and a life-like double-circle eye.

Tlaltecuhtli has the ritualistic function in Aztec religion of swallowing the sun and humans at dusk. According to Fraser this relates to the Aztec belief that the original gods must be repaid for having created man and preserved the universe. This repayment is achieved through human sacrifice and self-mortification (which renews the fertility of the earth), and the swallowing of the sun (which insures cosmic perpetuity).[4]

Tlaltecuhtli's counterpart, in Aztec belief, is the earth goddess Coatlicue,** who gave numerous attributes to Tlaltecuhtli: eagle talons which grasp the earth, a skirt of serpents which symbolizes earth, and the "skull god." Together they shared the dual role as creator of gods and men and as god (or goddess) of birth and death. (The NWC female bear ancestor's "abdominal mouth"—Fig. 57—is analogous in its symbolic function of rebirth and disaster.) The Aztecs believed, as did other primitive peoples, that from death or destruction comes new life. The duality implicit in the earth god—toad representing life; eagle,

---

*   A "skull god" is the underworld creature in charge of dead men's bones.

**   Tlazolteotl (see Fig. 22), the female counterpart of the male earth toad Tlaltecuhtli, has nearly the
       same associations as the female Coatlicue; therefore, we assume the female deities to be interchangeable.

side view top view

60. Image of a human face on an ornamented object. *Old Bering Sea Culture, 1000 B.C.–600 A.D. Ekven Cemetery, Chukchi Peninsula, Siberia. Walrus ivory, 6".*

joint mark

joint marks

joint marks

59. Crocodile god (?). Funerary Urn. *Marajo Island, Brazil.*

61. Chief with Tattoos* and gold ornaments. Vessel for ceremonial use. *Guanacaste, Nicoya Peninsula, Costa Rica 250–500 A.D. Redware pottery, orange-yellow, burnt sienna, dark brown, 5" or 24 cm.* Tattoos relate to crocodile-serpent cult.

the afterlife; and the skull-god being the intermediary, or death—is similar to that of the Thunderbird/Sisiutl combination (see p. 32), where the bird also symbolizes afterlife and the serpent, earthly life.**

---

*   Tattooing—see footnote with Fig. 73.

** Concepts from other cultures illustrate this duality. The Mayans thought of the earth as the back of a monstrous crocodile resting in a pool filled with water lilies. Earth's counterpart, the sky, was a double-headed serpent, a concept probably stemming from the fact that the word for sky was a homonym of the word for snake. The Mayans believed that all deities had two forms, day and night (see Fig. 50); the day-form (jaguar or sun) stood for life while the night-form reflected death.
The idea of dualism occurs, too, in a mythological character from New Ireland (Fig. 103) which also had two forms—male and female. In western society the male is often associated symbolically with the intellect, or spiritual life, and the female with the earth and material life.[5]

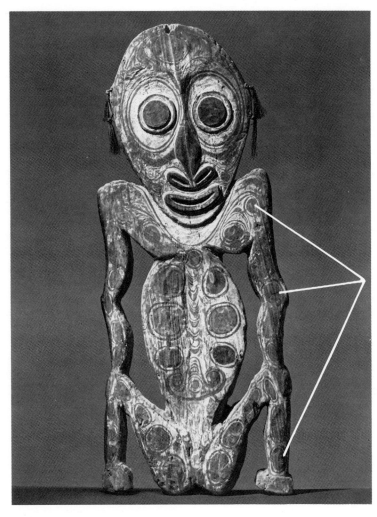

joint marks

62. **Splayed figure.**
*Sepik River, Lower region, New Guinea.
Wood, 57".*
The staring large eyes are further empha-
sized by the double circle eye motif repeated
over the body.

In the following examples from New Guinea, New Zealand, the Northwest Coast, Bering
Sea, and the Torres Strait, each artist has liberally used the **joint mark** motif as decorative
or filler device to create a rhythmic and unified design. Spirals are used as joint marks in
the Maori carving (Fig. 63).   In a bronze drum from China (Fig. 69) spirals are used pro-
fusely as space fillers and possibly as joint marks.

Occasionally, the use of joint marks might be compared to the Anglo-Saxon poetic
device known as "kenning" whereby a colorful metaphor is substituted for a common word:
"whale-road" for sea; "twilight-spoiler" for dragon. Perhaps the most remarkable example
of joint marks used metaphorically is seen in the "bear screen" (Fig. 57) in which a repeated face motif not only indicates the joints on the bear's arms and legs, but is strikingly
used to decorate the nose and eyes.

joint marks

three fingers of owl

63.   Ancestor figure.
      Part of the house Te-tau-ki-Turenga.
      Maori, by Ngati-Kaipoho at Monuteuke (Poverty Bay) 1846.

The house of which this panel is a part (Fig. 63) was once a ceremonial resting house for Maori ancestors and served as an assembly place for the living and dead. It represents the nucleus of *mana:* power or tribal prestige.[6]

Mana was a kind of psychic force or magical essence possessed by a tribe and safe-guarded by its warriors. The chief and his possessions were especially imbued with a "high-voltage" *mana.* The Maoris also believed that the artist worked under the tutelage of the gods, and therefore the more decorated an object, the more its *mana* or magical power.[7]

64. Frog coming out of his house.
Chief's dancing blanket.
Tlingit, NWC, recent copy.
Haines, Alaska.
*Hudson Bay Company blanket, navy blue with red
    felt border, fresh water clam shell buttons.*
59½" long, 67¼" wide, AIAI.

Emblem of Kiksodi clan, a subdivision of the Raven clan.

A young man was following a path in the woods. A frog was in the path ahead of him and he could not get around it. Since it was disrespectful to step over it, and the frog wouldn't budge, the young man turned back and told his story. The elders decided they wanted to be as unmovable as that frog, so they took it as their emblem.[8]

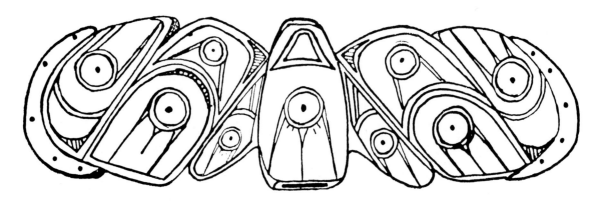

65. Winged object: balance for a whole harpoon.
Old Bering Sea or Obvik Culture, 1000 B.C.–600 A.D.
Pt. Hope, Alaska.
Fossil Ivory, 3½"(?).

The repeated double circles in this object can be taken as decorative but not necessarily as joint marks, since it is unclear exactly what this object represents artistically. When held vertically, the symmetrical wings of this harpoon balance resemble two bird profiles.* The fine Eskimo animal carvings of this era were highly variable and complex.

---

* In Eskimo carvings of this era the human head was typically elongated. Other winged objects (not illustrated) clearly show a human face in the central portion with an extended nose and perforated nostrils. (The perforation in the nostrils was for the sinew lashing the "wing" to the harpoon's basal socket. The harpoon is illustrated in Fig. 95.) The face may be surrounded by two animals, recalling the motif of the splayed figure flanked by two animals, and the double-headed serpent-with-face motif.[9]

66.   Owl (reinterpreted).
Woodcut on rice paper by Charles B. Greue.
Vancouver, British Columbia, 1953.
AIAI.

In Fig. 67 the added diamond-shaped decorations are referred to as eyes, and help Pijeba to lead the dead beneath the waters. Compare these to the Northwest Coast space filler devices on the chart in Fig. 11, with four different types of "eye" space fillers including a black eye! The Torres Strait eye "fillers" are used to decorate boats and help guide the boat safely.

Like Raven, of the NWC, Pijeba has the ability to turn himself into other forms. Pijeba may become a shark, lizard, or person leading the dead beneath the waters. As in the NWC culture, only those who have earned the right may wear this mask.

67.   Pijeba mask.
Torres Strait, Mabuiag Island, ca. 1885.
Tortoise shell, black with red and white, 4½" x 23"

The objects illustrated in this section, highly diverse in origin, possess a unique shared feature: **all are part-bird, part-human.** In several instances the bird-half is believed to act as guardian spirit to the human half; in other cases the bird represents an ancestor's soul, which can give power to the descendant-owner. Sometimes both characteristics apply. Notice the pervasive use of "bilateral split" as a design element. (See section on The Figure Split and Splayed.)

Bird depicted as guardian spirit		Bird depicted as ancestor's soul	
NWC (Salish),	Fig. 80	NWC (Salish),	Fig. 80
China (Shang),	Fig. 69	NWC (Chilcat),	Fig. 68
Arizona (Zuni),	Fig. 77	New Guinea	
Siberia (Perm),	Fig. 78	(Sepik River),	Fig. 72
Eskimo		Maori	Fig. 71
(Kuskokwin,		Siberia (Perm),	Fig. 78
Bering Sea),	Fig. 85	Eskimo (Kus-	
		kokwin,	
		Bering Sea),	Fig. 85

A widespread legend among Indian tribes is that thunder, lightning, and rain are caused by large birds, often called *thunderbirds.* * A Nootka Thunderbird legend:

> The mountain tops are lost in the clouds; they are melting away under an avalanche of hail and rain. Soon they will flow down the mountainsides in torrents of water and mud and boulders; they will flow down the rivers into the sea. The Thunderbird now flashes lightning. The mountains brighten once more; they stand high above the clouds. Behold the flashes! Behold the lightning! When the Eagle** spreads his wings over the valley, he loosens his Snake belt and whips the air with it. The shaft of lightning tears the sky asunder, and the thunderbolt hits the mountain peaks.[1]

An entry from a ship's log of 1790 recounts another version of how thunder is made:

> "They say it is particularly pleasing to their Deity to adorn a Whale with Eagles' feathers, for they suppose thunder is caused by conflicts between that Bird and the Fish. An Eagle of enormous size takes the Whale high in the air, and when it falls causes the noise of thunder . . ."[2]

---

* Inspiration for the Thunderbird idea is probably the giant condor, whose wingspread of 9½ feet exceeds that of any other Western Hemisphere bird. Only 40 or 50 condors are left in North America and, easily startled by man, are confined to isolated mountainous areas in southern California. The condor is a vulture which eats mostly carrion, has black plumage, a gray neck, and a reddish-orange head with glowing red irises in its eyes. A condor pair produces only one young bird every two years.

In South America another species of condor is depicted as an element of the Great Idol of Tiahuanaco, Bolivia (Figs. 93 and 94), and appears on ancient textiles from Peru's central coast (Fig. 118).

** Nootka legends interchange the characters of Eagle and Thunderbird quite freely.

Along the Northwest Coast many legendary adventures are attributed to Thunderbird, who is depicted in Fig. 68 as perched on Grizzly Bear. Here is one adventure:

In order to show uncultured man how to live better, Thunderbird assumed human form, built a community house, decorated it, and made fishing equipment and household objects. The possessions were guarded by Grizzly Bear.

As people passed by, Thunderbird invited them in to a great feast and showed them all he had. But when the guests left they dragged everything away, including Thunderbird himself. As they paddled home, a mammoth storm threatened to destroy them and their craft, but looking at their captured "host," they saw his eyes flash like lightning before each clap of thunder. Only then did they realize the connection between their unworthy act and their present predicament, and perceive that their host was Thunderbird disguised as a man. Promised protection from the storm if they turned from their churlish behavior, the men agreed to live in an enlightened way. Thunderbird, still in human form, married the daughter of a nearby chief. Until recent years their descendants erected Thunderbird totems to commemorate their famous ancestor.[3]

68.   Thunderbird perched on Grizzly
      Bear (his guardian).
      Chilcat, Northwest Coast.
      Wood, house paint, 7'.
      AIAI.

69. Drum with crocodile skin design on ends.
Shang or Chou Dynasty, China.
Bronze, 24½" w.

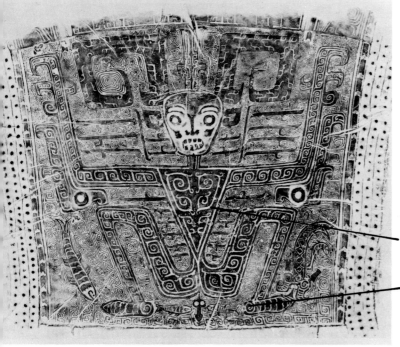

human being with guardian
spirit-winged headdress

note rib-like design

possible joint mark emphasis*

70. Rubbing of bird-man on the side of a bronze drum (above).

   Earliest of the Bird-man motifs used in this section is from the Shang Dynasty, China, about 1100 B.C. (Figs. 69 and 70). The object has a huge feathered headdress and is surmounted by a serpent and fish. (See Bird-Reptile Section.) A most appropriate place for this Chinese *"thunder*bird" is his location on a bronze drum (an earlier material was wood, which seems more practical!) The inscribed clan name (a curious carry-over from a pre-bronze age) is reminiscent of Northwest Coast totem usage, and that of other cultures, as is the association of the figure with guardian spirit beliefs.

---

* Also see double-circle visual metaphors, p. 56, and fret-hook motif, pp. 106–107.

72. **Figure and frigate bird (right.)**
Funeral Stele.
Sepik River, New Guinea, 1850.
Polychrome wood carving, snail shell eyes.
48" x 43¾"
The spirit of the deceased in the form of his totem animal, a frigate bird, is seen escaping through the head.

71. **(Recap of Fig. 34) Splayed figure,**
manaia **birds, with base of double headed snake.**
House lintel.
Maori, New Zealand, before 1867.
Wood, red paint, 3' x 1.5'.

Fig. 71, (a recap of Figure 34), a splayed figure flanked by two *manaia* (human-bird) creatures atop a two-headed snake, illustrates the "bird-man" concept in Maori culture. *Manaia*, an important symbol in Maori carving, is of obscure origin and assumes a half-human, half-bird character in many of its forms. Its association with the human image and its aggressive, vicious behavior suggests that it is a kind of demon or a "bird-reptile-human" god with a sinister nature.[4]

Another view sees *manaia* as the figure's personal spirit *(atua)* carrying the *mana* (power) of the ancestor it accompanies. *Manaia* is believed to be closely related to or to contain *mana*, an ancestor's magical and prestigious power. Thus, among the Polynesians, including the Maori,* birds are considered the medium of communication between the living and the dead.

This Polynesian bird-human association helps to account for the occurrence of bird-like traits on Maori human ancestral figures. The owl, in particular, is frequently illustrated. In Maori culture the owl is not only a carrier of spirits, but an "omen" bird as well. Owl eyes (legend, Fig. 51) and the three-claw bird "hands" and "feet" are elements of every splayed figure.**

Not illustrated are rock carvings on huge lava boulders of the Bird-Man (Tangatu Manu), a prehistoric bird cult at Orongo, Easter Island.

---

* The Maori migrated from the Cook or Society Islands to New Zealand around 1000 A.D.

** Another bird-related feature of Maori folklore is that the original food supply of the ancient Maori consisted largely of the flightless, now-extinct Moa bird, which once inhabited New Zealand in abundance.

73. Thunder*god*, Ibeorhum;
and two squirrels (?).
*Cuna Indians, Island of
Achutupu, San Blas Is-
lands, Panama, 19th C.
Mola:* cotton cloth ap-
pliqué with thread chain stitch.

Like Thunderbird, of the Northwest Coast, the Cuna Thundergod, Ibeorhum, is credited with teaching the people culture—how to build houses, conduct puberty ceremonies, picture-write, and worship.[5]   The Thundergod *mola* in Fig. 73 is not in the AIAI collection; but the *molas* which are share a similar emblematic, "early" style—not yet influenced by magazine illustrations, as is some contemporary Cuna work.

Molas evolved from 16th century body painting into painted abstract patterns on local "tree-cotton" material, used for a woman's loin cloth. (A return to body painting seems not improbable if Cuna artists persist in delving through outside magazines!)*   Beginning around the early 19th century, a newly married daughter could expect to receive a cotton hammock and painted loin cloths known as *makkalet picha*. From this developed the *Mukan mola* ("cloth of the grandmothers"), a cut-out appliqué of two layers, red and black. Later orange cotton trade material was made into a border on a red blouse. Gradually the number of layers increased, and the scope of decorative ideas opened up to include every-day objects such as animals and boats, and now even telephones and borrowed phrases like "GOOD HOUSEKEEPING." These days the *mola* is worn from under the arms to the waist in both the back and front. Each one represents about two months of work. The *mola* artist aims at distributing all colors evenly.[6]   Like the native craftsman of the Northwest Coast and of many other artistic traditions he seeks, often by exaggerating proportions, to fill space with lively decorative elements.

---

*   Body painting or tattooing was practised by Northwest Coast peoples, and by the Ainu (Japan), the Maori (New Zealand) and the Coclé people (Panama). The Cuna people are the only living descendants of the Coclé.

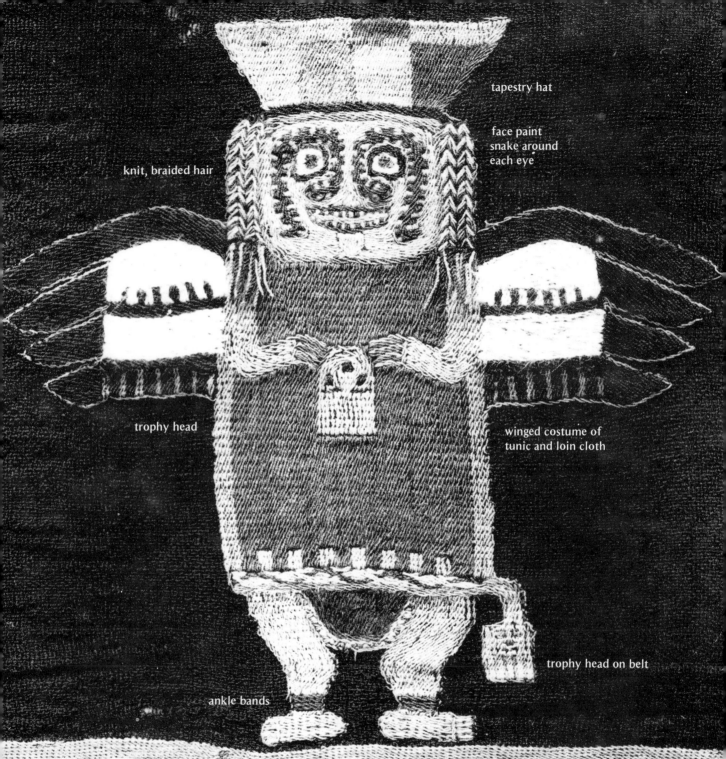

tapestry hat

face paint
snake around
each eye

knit, braided hair

trophy head

winged costume of
tunic and loin cloth

trophy head on belt

ankle bands

74. Winged man.
Mantle.
Late Paracas, Nazca 1B style, 400–200 B.C., Necropolis, Peru.
Alpaca dark grey-blue background; blue-green, navy blue, white, yellow, gold; cotton border stitch.

Both the figure and the border of the whole piece are outlined in rose red.

This Peruvian mantle shows a bird-man holding a "trophy-head" of a captured enemy. Another trophy head dangles from his belt. See trophy head cultures, p. 30.

painted face

75. **Dignitary with feather ritual vestment.**
    Ceramic plate.
    Mayan, 700–900 A.D.
    Campeche Coast, Mexico.
    Ochre, blue, red, black, 11¾".

Profile face with frontal body: a typical Mayan pose. See also Zapotec culture hero with quetzal feather headdress, Fig. 20.

Spattering technique performed Chinese-fashion, by means of the mouth.

76. **Man-eagle.**
    Clay food basin.
    Late Anasazi (ancient Pueblo), Sitkyatki, New Mexico.
    Pre-Columbian, 1400 A.D.

rainbow*

mountains

man-eagle

mountain lions with tail over back (x-ray view to guide arrow to animal's "soul")

It is interesting to note this man-eagle appears on a shield as protection.

77. Man-eagle.
Shield Design, "Priesthood of the Bow."
Zuni Indians, Arizona, U.S.A.
Skin.

The Ceremonial Legend Observed by a Zuni "Priest of the Bow:"

When travelling alone in country where danger from an enemy may be expected, a warrior takes out his fetish from the pouch and, scattering a pinch or two of sacred flour toward each of the four quarters** with his right hand, holds it in his left hand over his breast and kneels on the ground uttering this prayer:

> Si! This day, my fathers, ye animal gods, although this country be filled with enemies, render me precious. That my existence may not be in any way soever unexpectedly dared by the enemy, thus, shelter give ye to me from them! Long Tail (Mountain Lion), Knife-feathered (God of the Knife Wings), O, give ye shelter of my heart from them.

---

* The Kwakiutl (Northwest Coast) also portray the rainbow, in combination with Raven and Sisiutl.

** This reference to compass directions recalls Mayan beliefs in which four attendants to the priest represent the four directions.

The bird-man shaman's emblem from Perm, Siberia (Fig. 78 below), represents the shaman himself with Aiy, the eagle who came from the sun to bestow special powers on the first shaman. All shamans since then have descended from the first shaman; Aiy has taught them their powers and protected them. The Siberian shaman wears this emblem with a headdress consisting of a bird's head, eagle feathers representing his soul and creator Aiy, and a bird costume (which may show the bird's skeleton).[8]

On the Northwest Coast, many Kwakiutl legends tell of the gods of heaven sending an eagle to protect men from sickness and death. Because the people did not understand the message, the eagle transferred his powers to a man—the first shaman (see similar Salish legend, p. 69). Significantly, recent studies also report strong resemblances between northeast Siberian folklore and that of the (NWC) Tlingit and Tsimshian tribes.

The following items from Eskimo, Salish (NWC), New Guinea and New Ireland cultures seem to relate strongly, both visually and interpretively, to the shaman's emblem in Fig. 78. In Figs. 70, 77, 80, and 85, the bird element represents a protective and/or curative agent. Figs. 79, 80, 81, and 83 share the familiar protruding tongue motif (though in Fig. 80 the "tongue" is considered to be the bird's tail.)

78. Aiy, a Bird Protecting a Human Being. Shaman's emblem.
Perm, Russia (western Siberia).
Bronze.
Some Permian bronzes also have a double bird head like Salish mask (Fig. 83).

bird claw

mask face is *inua* (soul)

claws

bird's tail

79. **Spring Valley Ptarmigan Hunting Mask, with *inua* (soul).**
Eskimo, late 19th century.
Kuskokwim, Bering Sea, Alaska.
Wood and feathers; white, black and reddish brown paint, 15¾".

An *inua,* an inner, vital force believed to possess a human form, is depicted in order to propitiate it and ensure success in hunting or other activities.

Compare the arrangement of bird over face to that of the New Ireland Bird-man, Fig. 83.

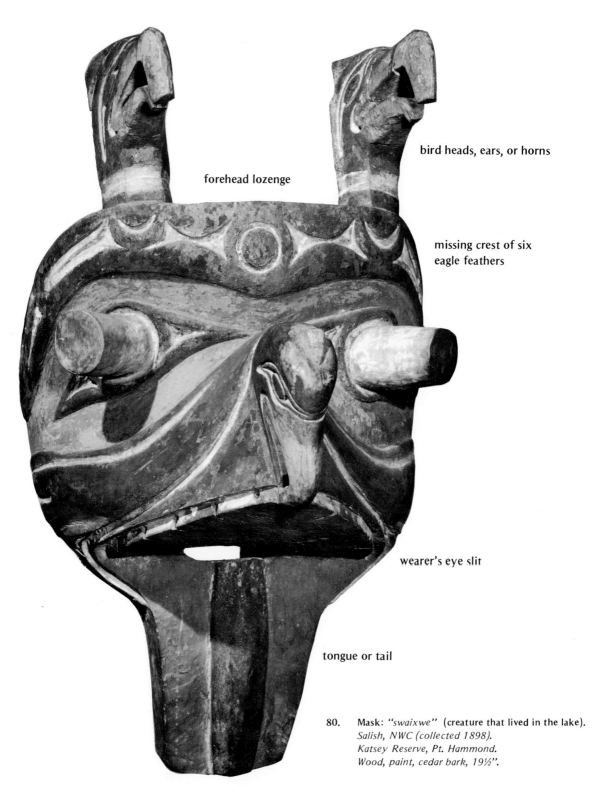

forehead lozenge

bird heads, ears, or horns

missing crest of six
eagle feathers

wearer's eye slit

tongue or tail

80.   Mask: "swaixwe" (creature that lived in the lake).
      Salish, NWC (collected 1898).
      Katsey Reserve, Pt. Hammond.
      Wood, paint, cedar bark, 19½".

The origin of the *swaixwe* mask is explained in the following Salish legend:

> An unhappy young man who suffered from a disgusting skin disease resolved to commit suicide. He went to a lake and attempted to drown himself, but instead of dying regained consciousness at the bottom of the lake finding that he had landed on the roof of a house. Upon entering it, he was greeted by the lake people who informed him that his spittle had caused illness among them. He effected a cure by stroking them with cedar bark and they in turn healed his skin ailment. After four days he returned to his village. There, he fetched his sister and they went to the lake where he had his fantastic adventure. She cast a line into the water, pulled it ashore and discovered the *swaixwe* mask and costume attached to it. Her brother became a powerful and fortunate man and promised to give his sister the mask upon her marriage.[9]

This legend says nothing to account for the bird-like features of the *swaixwe* mask, which was worn as part of a complete bird costume.* A strong link between the *swaixwe* mask and Siberian shamanism has been suggested, and this may help to explain the "bird" aspect of the mask. The Siberian shaman was inseparable from his Eagle protector and also wore bird-related clothing. Like the strong curative emphasis in the *swaixwe* legend, the shaman's chief function was healing, which he accomplished through his special association with animistic powers.

The *swaixwe* mask has two stylistic features which are interesting to compare with Chinese art. First, the *swaixwe* is jawless, like the *T'ao T'ieh* (Fig. 15).** Second, the association of peg eyes with protruding tongue are characteristic of much late Chou Chinese art.[10]† The **combination** of these stylistic parallels with the religious (shamanistic) similarities mentioned above seems to suggest again the absorption of some Asiatic influences into Northwest Coast art and culture.

---

*   The costume also included a swan feather ruff, feather breast plate and swan-skin leggings.

**   The bear in the Chilcat blanket (Fig. 15) is also jawless.

†   Fig. 83, a *Malanggan* man-snake-spirit bird mask, has a protruding tongue as well.

Note peg eyes, like
those of Salish mask.

protruding tongue

81.   Bird and man drum
     Sepik River, New Guinea
     Wood, 23.4"
     Convex tongue and bird
beak oppose the concave face,
rejoining the drum base.

70

82. **Sea monster mask.**
Kwakuitl, NWC.
Cape Mudge B.C., Canada.
Wood, bearskin, paint, twine, 5'9".

From a frontal view this NWC Kwakiutl mask (Fig. 82) has elements similar to the New Ireland bird-man-snake combination (Fig. 83); from top to bottom are seen Duck, Man's head, and Sea Monster. (Compare Thunderbird-splayed figure-Sisiutl mask, Fig. 35). The Sea Monster, *Gonaquadet*, actually consists of a Bear's head, with Sisiutl-like horns on a Killer Whale's body. The mask is used in spring ceremonies to scare salmon into shore.

(soul) bird

protruding tongue

A crested hair style, perhaps related to birds, was once common among inhabitants of New Ireland. The iconography of *Malanggan* masks is a clan secret known only to members of the clan.

See Fig. 79 for a similar Eskimo bird-man arrangement.

83. **Bird-man mask used in *Malanggan* ceremonies.**
New Ireland, 19th C.
Wood; red, yellow, black, blue colors introduced by Europeans, 37" x 21"

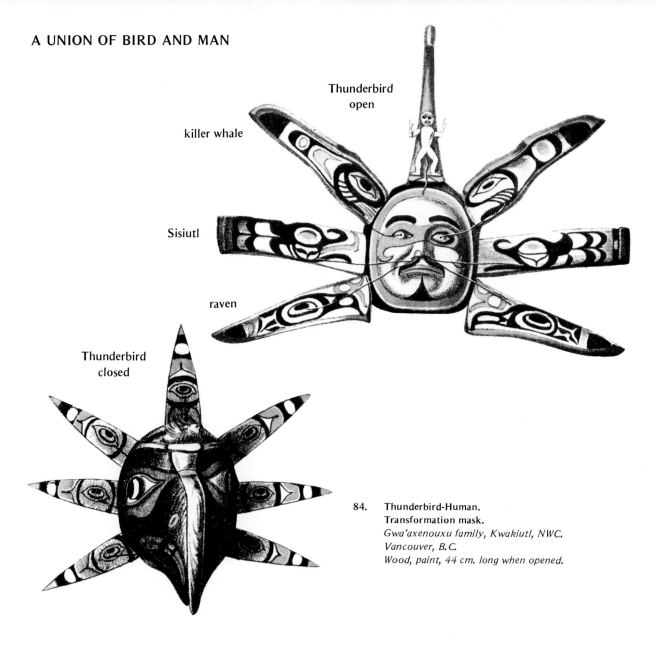

killer whale

Thunderbird
open

Sisiutl

raven

Thunderbird
closed

84.   Thunderbird-Human.
      Transformation mask.
      Gwa'axenouxu family, Kwakiutl, NWC.
      Vancouver, B.C.
      Wood, paint, 44 cm. long when opened.

The next two masks, instead of superimposing the bird above the man, employ a sophisticated and dramatic new device. The mask, with a pull of a string, opens up to reveal an inner face (NWC) or an inner soul (Eskimo). The **two-layer** device has been employed for Eskimo masks depicting a **human** being (Fig. 85); but in an Eskimo mask depicting an **animal,** one layer is adequate (Fig. 79), since the wearer inside is considered to embody the animal's spirit *(inua)*. Though the use of this pull-string mechanism seems confined to the Eskimo and Northwest Coast cultures, the transformation concept—one form hiding in or protected by another—underlies and unites almost all the bird-man examples in this section.*

---

*   Claude Levi-Strauss writes that an artistic motif, "four eyes of yellow metal," (referred to in a Chinese literary work, the "Impersonation of the Bear,") "recalls the multiple masks of the Kwakiutl and Eskimo."[11]

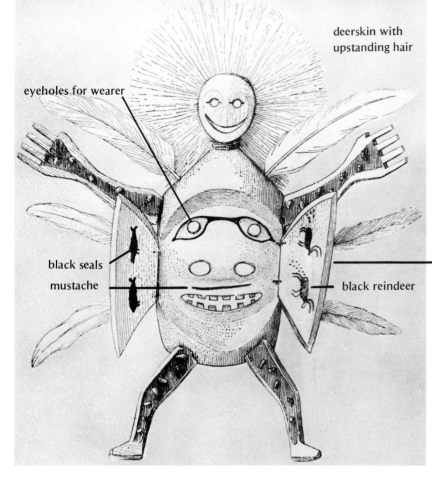

deerskin with
upstanding hair

eyeholes for wearer

Arms and legs represent
"mouth areas" (red with
black border) set with pegs
to represent teeth.

black seals

mustache

Doors reveal *inua* or inner vital
force believed to have a human
form.
The outer mask appears to protect the inner one, hiding the
hunter from the prey animal.

black reindeer

85.   Human figure with *inua*.
       Transformation Mask.
       Eskimo.
       Lower Kuskowin River, Alaska.
       *Wood, deerskin, paint: red,
          black, white, 11½" x 5".*

    The reindeer and seals on the "doors" of this mask (Fig. 85) probably act to strengthen
faculties such as sight, smell and hearing.[12]   This function is also attributed to objects on
the Tlingit Shaman's mask and on the Salish *swaixwe* mask (Fig. 80). The above Eskimo
mask (Fig. 85) might well have been used at an *Illigi,* a guest feast honoring the dead.
Illigi means throwing away, from the custom of giving everything away during the festival.
For four to six years before such an occasion all the participants—who may number as many
as two hundred and come from as many miles away—prepare by saving up valuable skins,
clothing and food.   Unlike the host of a Northwest Coast potlatch, the Eskimo host adopts
a humble mien, though his goal, too, is to give more gifts than his guests. The namesake
of the dead man honored by the feast is believed now to have the spirit of the deceased,
and receives presents whose ownership is attributed to the deceased.[13]

86.   "After Fishing," Koyokuk River
          Alaska.
       By Rusty Heurlin, 1957.
       AIAI.
       The Koyokuk River is a tribu-
tary to the Yukon River north of the
Kuskowin River (Fig. 85).
       This painting, in pastel tints,
shows an Eskimo returning home after fishing on an Indian summer day.

73

87.　Masked Kwakiutul dancers at a winter ceremony, photographed by E. S. Curtis in 1915.

Totem poles and Alaska. Instantly the mind joins these terms together. The association is valid, since totem poles once stood as an affirmation of a tribe's identity and ancestry, interspersed with cedar and spruce against the northern shoreline. Their craftsmanship is a blend of the strength and sensitivity which are hallmarks of Northwest Coast wood carving.

Totem poles, of course, were not exclusively Alaskan, but extended well down along the Canadian coast, and were a feature of most Northwest Coast peoples. A glance at this section will show, too, that carved wooden poles (which we shall informally call "totem"* poles) are characteristic of many Pacific Basin cultures.

Totemism is defined as "an association between groups of people and some animal, plant, or inanimate object." (Webster). It is not hard to see how this concept can apply to almost any culture. (The word *totem* itself is thought to be of Ojibway [North American Indian] origin. Anglo-Saxon names such as Foxx, Wolfe, Drake and Steere (and their coats of arms) hint at an early acceptance of totemic beliefs among our European forebears. Relics of this ancient association may be seen in the frequent adoption of animal names by athletic and civic groups, not to mention sub-groups of the Cub Scouts.

Totem poles visually commemorate ancestor and/or animal guardians. The poles are used to mark graves, show off rank, or just stand alone in memory. Despite rumors to the contrary, they are not meant to tell a story but to act as memory devices (see discussion of the "ordering of society" on page 11).

Remarkable similarities in such aspects as symmetry, frontality, and the use of space fillers can be seen in totem poles from diverse places. (Of course, the fact that the totem pole is a *pole* may restrict the design possibilities and reinforce the similarities.) The head size of major characters is exaggerated in most totem poles, emphasizing achieved status.** In the NWC totem pole in Fig. 88, vertical features such as tall hats and folded wings fill the space between the main characters. The figures tend to interlock. Notice how the Raven's wings encompass a Frog standing on top of a man's potlatch hat.

---

*   See ** footnote, p. 10.

**   See discussion of Zapotec culture hero, p. 23.

Tall "basket-woven" hats* symbolize high prestige, earned through three previous potlatches.

three nephews of Raven

Raven

frogs**

Grizzly Bear-of-the-sea with protruding tongue, emblem of William G. Jeffrey

88.   View front and side.
      Raven ("Lahk-seh-el") Totem Pole.
      By William G. Jeffrey.
      Git-wil-gyots Tribe, Tsimshian, NWC, 1965.
      Prince Rupert, British Columbia.
      Wood and house paint, 10'.
      AIAI.
      A contemporary Tsimshian chief, William Jeffrey, carved the pole and, contrary to male tradition, he used a design by his daughter, Princess Little Ice.

This totem pole recalls one story of creation:

During the flood the Raven has been flying and carrying his three nephews† (top of totem pole). Weary of his burden, he sees an object in the desolate ocean. It is Frog, in a gigantic state, looking like an island. He calls out to Frog, "Help me, for I am weak with fatigue. We will all perish and there will be none left alive." Frog agrees to let them rest on his broad back till the floods subside. In this way the nephews were rescued and their tribe saved from extinction.[1]

---

*   These hats are thought by Marius Barbeau to be of Mongolian origin.[2]

**   Frogs are frequently seen on shamans' objects, suggesting that they are potent spirit helpers.[3]

†   Under the matrilineal NWC custom, maternal nephews become the heirs-apparent.

The raven, with his sleek, black coat, is a common sight along the Northwest Coast. NWC peoples regarded him as a culture hero and depicted him as an audacious trickster whose pranks had far-reaching effects. One Tlingit legend tells of Raven as the Transformer and Creator who brought light into the world:

The light was kept in the house where a supernatural being and his daughter lived. To gain access to the house Raven transformed himself into an evergreen needle and, when the daughter dipped her cup in the nearby stream to drink, he floated into the cup. Suspecting a trick, the girl flicked the needle out of the cup. The next day when the girl came to drink, Raven entered her cup as a tiny grain of sand. She drank the water and, unwittingly, the grain of sand. Soon thereafter she bore a child—Raven in disguise. As the child grew, he would cry until his "grandfather" gave him the sun, which was kept in a box in the corner of the house. He was allowed to play with the sun, but at night he put it back in the box. One night Raven, turning back into a bird, took the sun out of its box and tried to fly through the smoke hole in the roof. The flames leaped at him, blackening his coat. The grandfather, awakened by the commotion, tried to catch him and almost succeeded because the weight of the heavy sun forced Raven to fly low. To unburden himself Raven broke off chunks of the sun and tossed them into the sky. Smaller pieces became the stars, and a large piece became the moon. Then Raven threw what remained of the sun into the sky and escaped to earth. This was how Raven became black and the earth lost its blackness, having instead the stars, the moon, and the sun.[4]

89. "Raven and the Daughter of the Nass" #1.
By Dale De Armond.
Juneau, Alaska, 1963.
Woodcut, AIAI.

This Kigiktauik (Eskimo) legend resembles in part the Tlingit version of how light came to the world:

After Raven realized he had unwittingly created man, who dropped from a pea pod which Raven had made, he directed the way man should live. But man killed too many animals, and as punishment Raven took away the sun. Raven's older brother took pity on the people, pretended to die and became a fallen leaf which Raven's wife ate. She soon produced a male offspring which pestered Raven for the sun to play with. The young raven (Raven's brother in disguise) was given the sun, and he threw it back into the sky, giving the world light once more.[5]

top knot of hair
(Northwest Coast men
also wore their hair in
a bunch at the top of
their heads.)

90.   Colossal Tiki (human ancestor) Cenotaph.
Raroera Pak, Maori, New Zealand.
Wood.
   This memory pole (cenotaph) of the
daughter of a great chief is carved from a
single tree.

   Both the Northwest Coast peoples and the Maori "read" the poles from top to bottom
in a time sequence from ancient to modern.   The bottom element often represents the
owner of the totem.

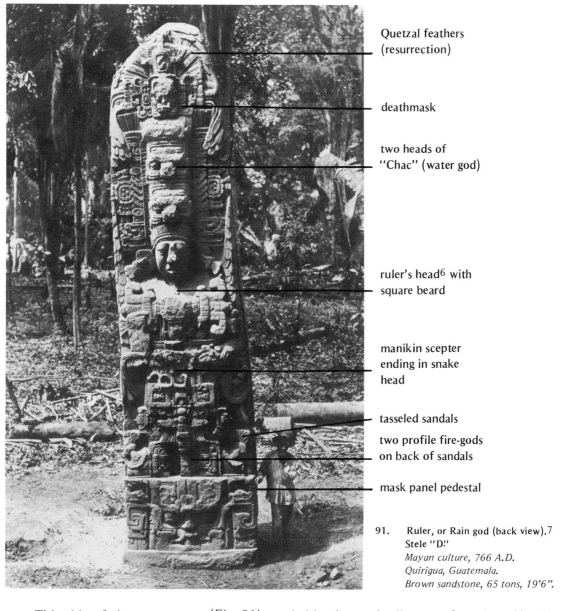

Quetzal feathers
(resurrection)

deathmask

two heads of
"Chac" (water god)

ruler's head[6] with
square beard

manikin scepter
ending in snake
head

tasseled sandals

two profile fire-gods
on back of sandals

mask panel pedestal

91.   Ruler, or Rain god (back view).[7]
       Stele "D."
       Mayan culture, 766 A.D.
       Quirigua, Guatemala.
       Brown sandstone, 65 tons, 19'6".

This side of the monument (Fig. 91), probably shows the lineage of a ruler. Heavily loaded with ornaments, it suggests that the office matters more than the man. This Classic Period ruler looks dignified and formal, constrained within the mummy-like rectangle.

On the sides (not illustrated) of this massive limestone sculpture are intricate glyphs (picture writing) commemorating a five-year period at Quirigua. Only partially deciphered, the glyphs relate to the calendar and gods "in astrological combinations for purposes of prophecy and divination."[8] The glyphs on Stele D are considered the finest of the entire Mayan era.

92.   Great Idol: Pachamama—goddess of food-giving earth.
        (front and back views).
      Gateway to Temple of Sun
      Tiahuanaco, Peru; moved to La Paz, Bolivia.
      Red sandstone. 19'6" high, 5' wide. 1000 A.D.
        Portions of this statue were badly damaged in
1894, when it was used as a target for rifle practice by
the Bolivian army.

93.   Copies of Great Idol.
       Bolivia.
       Wood, 2½'.
       AIAI.
       These figures are simplified
copies, in miniature, of the 19½
foot high Great Idol of Tiahuanaco
(Fig. 92). Each holds a Pacific Condor, thought to be the inspiration
for the mythical Thunderbird. (See
discussion of Condor, p. 57.)

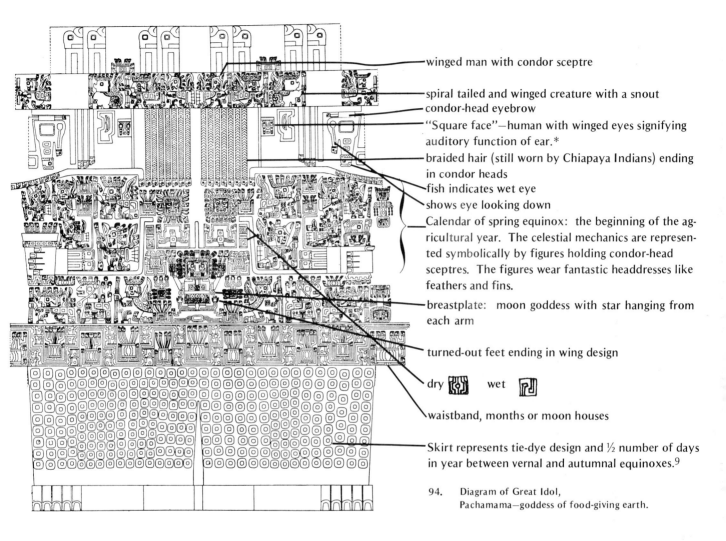

winged man with condor sceptre

spiral tailed and winged creature with a snout
condor-head eyebrow
"Square face"—human with winged eyes signifying auditory function of ear.*
braided hair (still worn by Chiapaya Indians) ending in condor heads
fish indicates wet eye
shows eye looking down
Calendar of spring equinox: the beginning of the agricultural year. The celestial mechanics are represented symbolically by figures holding condor-head sceptres. The figures wear fantastic headdresses like feathers and fins.
breastplate: moon goddess with star hanging from each arm
turned-out feet ending in wing design

dry   wet

waistband, months or moon houses

Skirt represents tie-dye design and ½ number of days in year between vernal and autumnal equinoxes.⁹

94.   Diagram of Great Idol,
Pachamama—goddess of food-giving earth.

The impressive art and architecture of Tiahuanaco, which influenced later Peruvian coast cultures, was situated on Lake Titicaca in the bleak highland of western Bolivia. The Great Idol was part of this architectural complex which gave pre-European America the most accurate calendar of its time.** The surface of the huge statue is a rich bisymmetrical organization of symbolic figures and animals relating to the calendar. H. S. Bellamy proposed that the calendar is the world's oldest, "built," as he put it, "before the flood" —and much earlier than the 1000 A.D. date usually attributed to the culture. Pursuing the theory propounded by Hans Hoerbiger, Austrian cosmologist, Bellamy suggested that the glyphs corresponded to another geologic era when the earth had a prominent equatorial "water girdle" influenced by a satellite which preceded the moon.¹⁰

*   Compare this square head with the Northwest Coast filler device on the Chilcat blanket, pp. 15 and 16.

**   The Mayan Stele "D" (Fig. 91) with its glyphs also served as a calendar; and some huge Toltec (Mexican) idols (not shown) have a calendar function.

The winged object in Fig. 65 might fit here.

A.

bird-like beak or nose

mouth

95.   Harpoon foreshaft (Item A) and harpoon.
      Socket pieces (Items B and C)
      Old Bering Sea Style, 1000 B.C.–600 A.D.
      Ekven Cemetery, Chukchi Peninsula, Siberia.

B.   C.

This harpoon shaft assembly is included in the "Totem Pole" section because of its intricate interlocking shapes.* Compare the eagle-wing-like arrangement of this Siberian object with the style of a close neighbor, the Northwest Coast Raven totem pole in Fig. 88. The interlocking shapes may indicate a ceremonial significance. Compare also the face-like design on pieces B and C to the Maori curvilinear figures (Fig. 108).

Like Northwest Coast tribes, people of the Old Bering Sea culture had totem marks *(alhinuk)*. Weapons marked with an animal totem are believed invested with some of the aspects of the animal represented and endowed with a special lethal quality.

96.   Arctic Whale Hunt.
      By Rusty Heurlin.
      Oil painting, 41" x 28",
      1955.
      AIAI.
      The Nootka, alone among the Northwest Coast Indians, were whale hunters. Both the Nootka and the people of the Old Bering Sea culture used harpoons with detachable shafts and long lines of whale sinew.
      Ritual songs gave magical powers like those of lightning to the Nootka harpoons.[11]

*   The harpoon shaft has burial significance, as Northwest Coast totem poles sometimes do.

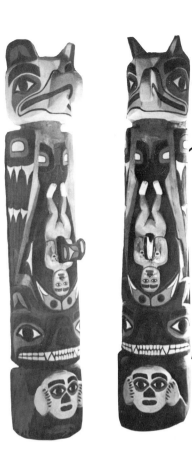

Owl, seer for Wackhayea
and Git-wil-gyots tribe

Killer Whale

Whale is often depicted carrying
a departed soul to the grave or
underworld, not unlike the boat
transport used for that purpose
in other cultural traditions.

Sea Grizzly Bear holding
human head symbolizing
clan members of Git-wil-
gyots tribe. Mr. Jeffrey
describes Grizzly as the
"mother of us all" and
"lord of his domain."

97.   Owl, Killer Whale, Sea Grizzly Bear ("Gispewudwade") Totem Pole.
      William Jeffrey.
      Git-wil-gyots tribe, Tsimshian, Northwest Coast, 1965.
      Prince Rupert, British Columbia, Canada.
      Wood and House paint, 10'.
      AIAI.

The Tsimshian legend of Wackhayea:[12]

Wackhayea, an interior Indian warrior with supernatural powers, became espoused to a Tsimshian maiden. With his three brothers-in-law he practised for the important sea lion hunt. After the winter rains they set out for the big hunt. Upon reaching their destination, strong winds made the rocks extremely slippery, and the four men became quite fearful.

Then Wackhayea volunteered to climb onto the island where the great sea lions were. His brothers-in-law taunted him: "Who are you—you are from the interior and know only how to be a woodsman." But he replied, "Why, I could pigeon toe over those rocks with my snow shoes!"

On the fourth breaker, he easily alighted onto the island. Two of the three brothers were infuriated, and decided to leave him there, though the youngest protested in vain. When they returned home, they told their sister that her husband had perished in the storm.

Meanwhile, Wackhayea had killed as many sea lions as the party needed and fell into a deep slumber on the rocky island. He thought he was dreaming when he heard a little voice saying, "My grandfather is inviting you." He sat up and saw a little mole running into a thick growth of grass. Lifting the grass, he saw a ladder going down to a huge underground dwelling, and he soon found himself in the interior of a grand lodge. At the far end was the chief. Knowing of Wackhayea's supernatural powers, the chief implored him, "Oh, miracle man, cure my son!"

Wackhayea replied, "On this one condition: that you assist me in returning home."

The chief said, "I shall fulfill my promise to send you home and all my people will witness this."

Wackhayea noticed that most of the people there had arrows embedded in their flesh. First Wackhayea attended to the chief's son and removed the arrow which was torturing him, and he did the same for the others. Afterward the chief held a great feast during which he spoke of his happiness that his people had been restored. Then Wackhayea realized that the people he had helped were actually sea lions disguised as humans.

The chief gave Wackhayea a huge canoe and instructed him, when he reached the surface, to climb into it and call out "Oh! westerly wind, blow me homeward." But Wackhayea did not return to the village of his wife. He was set on vengeance against the brothers who had left him to die on the island. He carved huge killer whales out of wood. Using his supernatural powers, he commanded them to kill the two older brothers, but to spare the youngest, who can now be seen riding on the back of killer whale on the totem pole. It was in this way that these whales became known as Killer Whales.

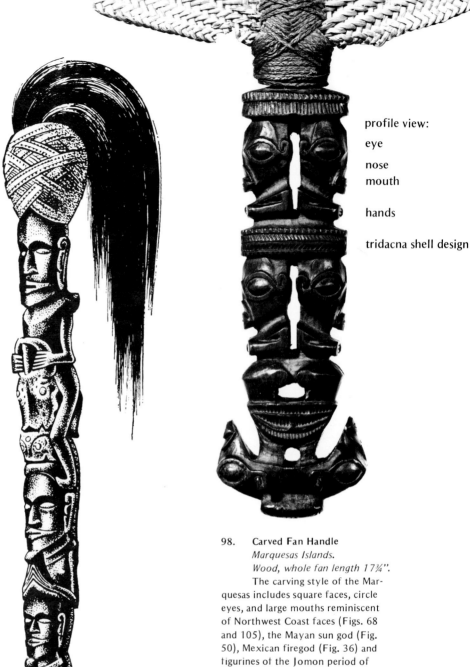

profile view:

eye

nose

mouth

hands

tridacna shell design

This upside down → animal has similarities to Northwest Coast Killer Whale, Fig. 97. A Northwest Coast shaman had a staff, as did the host of a ceremonial occasion, who carried it as a badge of office.

98.   Carved Fan Handle
      Marquesas Islands.
      Wood, whole fan length 17¾".
      The carving style of the Mar-
      quesas includes square faces, circle
      eyes, and large mouths reminiscent
      of Northwest Coast faces (Figs. 68
      and 105), the Mayan sun god (Fig.
      50), Mexican firegod (Fig. 36) and
      figurines of the Jomon period of
      Japan (not illustrated).

99.   Shaman's staff, consisting of a series of ancestors.
      Toba Batak tribe.
      Sumatra, Indonesia.
      Wood, 67" full length approximately.

Each of the carvings in Figs. 97 through 100 includes an interesting **upside-down** feature.

100. Post of rank.
Malekula, New Hebrides.
Tree root fern. 4.3'.

The arms of the upper figure become the eyebrow ridge of the lower.

This upside down figure works nicely as the headdress of the lower figure.

head upside down

101. Ancestor figures.
New Hebrides.

Note on either side of the room are poles with arrangements of mythical characters.

tridacna shell

for the placement of the carver's payment   detail (Fig. 103) next page   detail (Fig. 104)

102.   Cult House with *Malanggans*.
       Medina, New Ireland.
       Wood, bamboo, palm and croton leaves.
       Figures: soft wood, earth pigments and
                   yellow oil color.
       House: H. 8', L. 16'4", D. 10'.

This men's cult house in New Ireland was erected to commemorate a *malanggan.*
    Here fourteen deceased persons from the village were honored by these sculptures and accompanying dances, chants, speeches and feasts, lasting over several months.

    A *malanggan* may also serve as an initiation into manhood and, like the Northwest Coast potlatch, is always an important means of enhancing the organizer's prestige.

    The carvings (also called *malanggan*) represent mythological events, ancestors, totem animals, and symbols of the sun and moon. They were carved in secret by male descendants who proclaimed in long speeches their right to make them.

    Art historians regard Northwest Coast Indian art and the *malanggan* style of Northern New Ireland as the apexes of North and South Pacific art respectively.

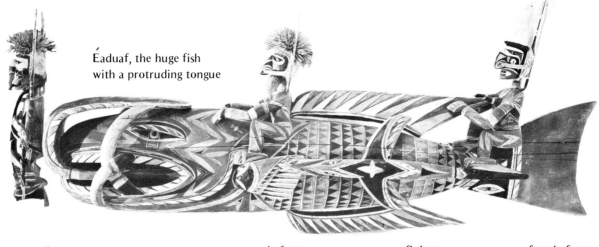

Éaduaf, the huge fish
with a protruding tongue

| man-god: Lamesisi | snake | male form of Solauang | flying fish | female form of Solauang |

male and female aspects

woman who fills
water gourds
and gives water
to protector-birds

103. Detail of Cult House *Malanggan*, containing
Éaduaf (the fish) and mythical characters.
Medina, New Ireland. 270 cm.
Other *Malanggan* figures appear in Fig. 83.

fish tail fins

legendary man
who died after
having stepped
on a fish

104. *Malanggan* mast, Cult House detail.
Wood and bamboo, 7' 5½''.

fish's head

large central figure is Rain god

border figures: "raindrops splash up"

Detail of Figure 105, page 89. The entrance hole is covered with goatskin.

Totem posts are used architecturally by five Pacific Basin cultures. Examples from three cultures are illustrated here: Northwest Coast, Maori, and Siberia.

Unillustrated is the use of the double-headed serpent-demon* with a protruding tongue used on sacred houses or tombs by the Northwest Coast people, by the Maori (serpent called Marakihau), by the Dayak of Borneo (serpent known as Naga Trebang), by the Batak of Sumatra,[13] and by the Chinese, where the motif appears as connected but diverging dragon heads on I-Nan tomb (pre-Han, 205 B.C.).[14]

---

*   Also see architectural uses of the double-headed snake, p. 40.

left post, symbolizing tree where
Woodworm lived: Girl, Woodworm,*
Crane holding Frog who lived in
roots of tree

right post:
Raven standing on Salmon

huge potlatch dish of Woodworm

105. Whale House interior screen with hole to Chief's apartment.
      Chilcat, subtribe of Tlingit (artist was Tsimshian).
      Klukwan, Alaska. 20' x 9½' h.

Houses on the Northwest Coast were built to accommodate as many as fifty people.
The chief and his family lived in the warm back section, partitioned off and perhaps slightly raised. Ceremonies and public gatherings were held here. Seldom was there an exclusive
structure for social or religious functions.

Interior walls and supporting posts were beautifully carved and painted. Often two
poles situated in the middle of the house, directly behind the fire, marked the chief's seat
of honor.

—————————

*   Woodworm, suckled by the chief's daughter as her child; now a clan emblem.

106.   Tribal house of Chief Shakes, with Gonaquadet and
        grizzly mortuary poles and bear screen.*
        Tlingit, copy.
        Wrangell, Alaska, on original site of Wrangell Island.
        Wood.

three toads:
ridicule pole,
debt unpaid

*   Original bear screen, Figure 57.

107. Chief Shakes, head of the Killer Whale Totem Clan of the Tlingit Indians, with ceremonial objects.

top knot of hair

large brows

staring eyes of
abalone shell insets

averted nostrils

tongue—a sign of defiance

108. Rua (First Woodcutter)
      under protecting ancestor.
      Maori, New Zealand.
      Wood house.

92

This ceremonial "totem" house (Fig. 92) is a resting place for the spirits of dead Maori ancestors who take an active interest in the affairs of the tribe. The house was a traditional meeting place for the living and the dead, and thus the focal point of tribal prestige, or *mana.* *

The wooden structure is made to represent the body of a primal ancestor: its rafters were ribs, its ridgebeam a spine, its frontal boards outstretched arms, and its pinnacle a mask-face.

Rua,** the legendary first woodcarver of the Maori tribe, was a reputed half deity who could perform supernatural acts. This is how Rua acquired his fame.

> Rua's son, while sailing one day, was captured by the sea-god Tangaroa and taken to Tangaroa's sea-floor house. Rua, frantically searching for his son, eventually discovered him in Tangaroa's house which he entered only after conspiring with the doorkeeper. Once inside he was delighted to find carven images talking to each other. Rua later hid himself outside the house until Tangaroa and his attendants entered to sleep for the night. The next morning Rua "set fire" to the house, that is, allowed rays of sunlight to enter, a thing greatly abhorrent to Tangaroa and his household, and stood at the door striking down each member of the household as they emerged to escape the unwanted light.

> Rua then returned to the world with his rescued son, bringing also the carvings which he saved from the "sun-flames," Interestingly enough, the ones which he selected were those that could not speak. The legend says that had Rua selected those carvings with the power of speech, "the posts of houses (such as the one depicted) would still have the ability to talk."[15] These carvings, then, served as models for Rua's later work and for the men who followed him in the art of woodcarving. An old proverb sums up Rua's achievement in these words: "The art of carving is the art of Rua."[16]

---

*   Concept of *mana*, discussed previously. See page 55 (Fig. 63).

**   An important reference to the stories of Rua and related tales is the collection of myths and legends by A. W. Reed, entitled *Treasury of Maori Folklore.*

109. Tomb.
*Ghilyak, Eastern Siberia,
    19th century.
Wood.*

This Eastern Siberian burial house is like some Haida burial houses. Very likely the design of the Haida structures was derived from early Russian contacts. Walking through a graveyard from either culture is like walking through a miniature village of doll or dog houses; those of the Haida are carved and decorated with Northwest Coast totem animals.

110. Tokyo Lion's Club Totem.
*Ueno Park, Tokyo, Japan, 1950.
Cement.*

This garish Japanese "totem pole" with the tiger's red protruding tongue may be taken, tongue in cheek, as an example of modern-day cultural diffusion.

94

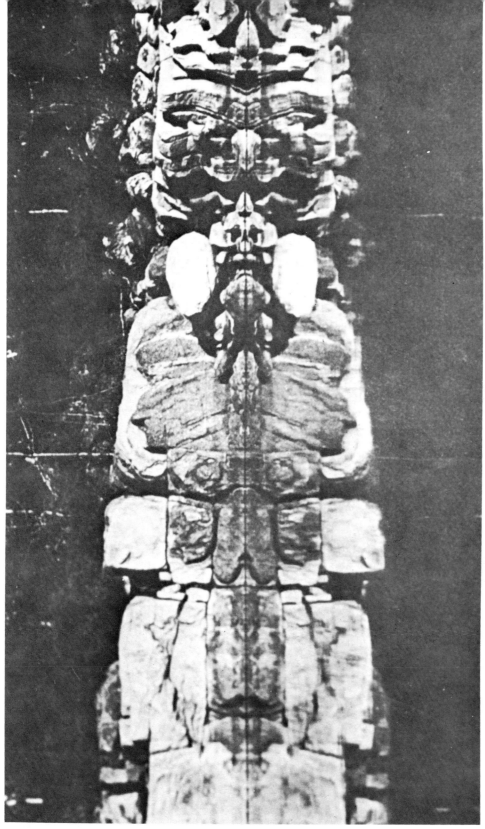

111. Give this "totem pole" a right-angle turn, and its identity
 is revealed: a rocky shore reflected in still water.

 # BURIAL ITEMS

The items in this section are quite heterogeneous in design and origin, but most are related in some way to burial customs or procedures—either as commemorative markers, burial containers, burial wrappings, or prestige items which are ritually interred with the deceased. Several items, though having no particular burial significance, are included because of their similar decorative motifs.

The towering wooden poles which most people associate with the Northwest Coast stood detached from other structures and were purely commemorative. Since it is known that the availability of metal tools and manufactured paints stimulated the production of this type of totem pole,* it seems plausible that the huge poles may not have been so commonplace before European contact. Functional types of poles such as house posts, grave markers, cremation posts or shaman's staffs were probably more numerous. Some of these, such as the Haida grave marker in Fig. 112, were of quite modest dimensions. The grave slab from Costa Rica (Fig. 113), made of stone, is illustrated here because of its comparable design and its function of commemorating ancestors.

---

*   See p. 106, center pole.

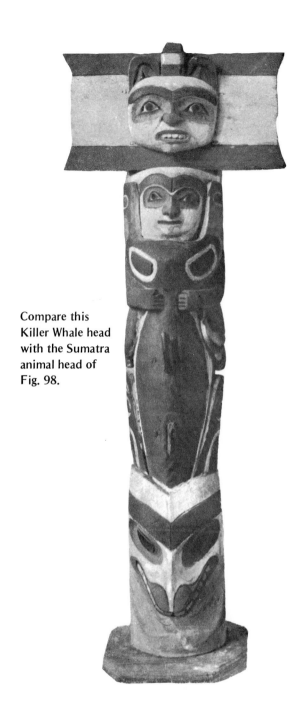

Compare this
Killer Whale head
with the Sumatra
animal head of
Fig. 98.

112. Grave marker: face of Tcamaos (personification
      of the "snag" or "tide-walker"), holding Killer
      Whale.
      Haida, Northwest Coast.
      Skidegate, British Columbia.
      Wood, paint: white, red, black, blue-gray, orange.
      37½".

113. Grave slab of matrilinear clan (showing
      guardian spirits).
      Reventazon area, Costa Rica, pre-Columbian,
      * 900 A.D.*
      Stone.
      Approx. 80".

ears

Bear's body
(head filler on stomach)

fins

raven?

bear

114. Grizzly Bear burial* or storage chest.
*Chief Shakes',** Tlingit, Northwest Coast, 1850.
Wood and paint: red, black, blue, white.
36" x 20¼" x 21-7/8".*

According to Claude Levi-Strauss, a Northwest Coast chest is not merely a container embellished with a painted or carved animal. It **is** the animal itself (or was so regarded by its owners) keeping active watch over the contents which have been entrusted to its care.[1]

The bear depicted on the chest in Fig. 114 is "Skoo-d-cheet," the Grizzly—an important clan emblem, indicated by the fin on either side of the head. (The house screen of the Shakes family in Fig. 57 depicts a **brown** bear.) Here is a bear legend recounted by the Shakes family:

> A hunter was captured by a grizzly bear, which threw him into his den. The she-bear, instead of destroying him, concealed him, and, when the grizzly came around, denied that the hunter was ever thrown into the cave. The male grizzly went away never to return. The hunter then married the bear and had children by her, though he already had a wife and children living in his village. He hunted for his bear wife and children. Finally he had a longing to return to his house, and the bear gave him permission but warned him not to have anything to do with his wife. When he reached the village, his wife reproached him for leaving her alone so long a time. He began to hunt for them. The bear heard of this and became very jealous. The next time the hunter was found in the woods, she directed her cubs to fall on him and kill him, and they did.

---

*   See coffin on a mortuary pole, Fig. 49.

**   See other Chief Shakes items, Figs. 57, 105, 106, 107.

A box such as the one illustrated in Fig. 114 was typically constructed with all four sides fashioned from one continuous piece of wood, which has been kerfed and bent into shape. The bottom and top are added as separate pieces. Like a painting or a Chilcat blanket (see Fig. 12), the relatively flat surface of a box tends to favor abstract decoration in contrast to the more recognizable animal forms, sculptured in deep relief, on totem poles. The whole design of this box is gently curved (unlike that of the blanket), avoiding excessive parallelism within the rectangular form.

The strong, beautiful carving of the chest in Fig. 114 (not adequately revealed by the lighting in the photograph) is so strikingly similar to the carving styles of the next two figures (ritual vessels from China and from the Mayan Culture) that they are here presented, though they probably had nothing to do with *burial* traditions!

See related design on a funerary urn from Marajo Island, Brazil (Fig. 59).

115. **Hu, (ritual wine vessel).**
Chou, China, 900–650 B.C.
Bronze, with lid, 21-1/8".

116. **Jaguar ritual vessel.**
Late Classic Mayan Culture.
Ulua Valley, Honduras, 800–1000 A.D.
Calcite, 10".

THE BURIAL CONTEXT

Traditional burial customs among Northwest Coast tribes were astonishingly diverse, considering the many striking artistic and cultural similarities. The body might be put in a carved box (Fig. 114) and placed on a pole (Fig. 49) or in the trees;* it might be put in the ground (denoted by grave marker, Fig. 112); or in a miniature Haida "doll house" structure. The three northern NWC tribes (Haida, Tlingit, Tsimshian) preferred cremation, often inserting the ashes into the back of a totem pole; though sometimes, as among the Tsimshian, the body (probably that of a shaman) was mummified.

Along the Central Coast of Peru some groups also used the last technique, and for this purpose produced carved and painted boxes, wrapping the mummies in beautiful tapestry cloth. Two well-preserved examples of Peruvian "Mummy bundles," illustrated in Figs. 117 and 118, are part of the AIAI collection. These 13th century A.D. fragments stem from a four thousand-year tradition of Peruvian textile weaving before the Spanish conquest. During this time techniques and motifs were extremely persistent; some design elements can be traced through practically the entire time-span. With very simple equipment such as the backstrap loom, weavers achieved high quality and diverse effects through varied techniques. The extreme dryness of coastal Peru, similar to the climate of Egypt, has preserved a surprising number of relatively fragile objects such as the textiles pictured here from the AIAI collection.

These designs make use of positive and negative space: the "background" turns out to be another design just as interesting as the one first catching your eye.

---

* This was also a northern Maori custom.

117. Pelican motif.
Mummy bundle, textile fragment.
Central Coast, Peru, 1200–1500 A.D.
Cotton; red, yellow, light brown, white.
7½" x 13½". AIAI.

THE BURIAL CONTEXT

118. Step-block, fret-hook, and pelican motifs.
Mummy bundle, textile fragment.
Central Coast, Peru, 1200–1500 A.D.
Cotton, brown and white, 3½" x 14½" (fringe extra).

A. Abstract condor head (see Thunderbird, Page 57)
on background of alternating brown and white
diagonal stripes

B. Step-block motif, white-line details

C. Fret hook (spiral), thick-thin, slightly diagonal
direction. Spiral becomes geometric fret hook

D. Brown pelicans

E. Horizontal areas a. diagonal step-block, fret hook,
        square
     b. white or brown stripe
     c. pelican

F. Fret-hook, outlined square

G. Diagonal line step, diagonal line, outlined square

H. Diagonal areas a. interlocking rounded fret-hook
     b. diagonal step-block, positive,
        negative
     c. abstract pelican head
     d. bird body

I. Reflected pelican motif

A

B

C

D

E

F

G

H

I

Using only two colors, brown and white, and a very limited number of motifs spaced vertically, horizontally, or diagonally, the artist has achieved great diversity. Within the eight sections from top to bottom a pelican, or pelican head, highly stylized, appears in sections A, B, D and E. In section A the brown pelican is mirror-imaged against a white abstract design. Note how the simple diagonal step-block motif is employed in varied forms uniting almost every section. It is used boldly as part of the pelican's wing and tail; in miniature it defines the bird's neck and beak.

Weaving Information[2]

Both figures: Backstrap loom. Details achieved through finger skills. (NWC weavers used a twining method.)

Figure 117:   "Double cloth"; black and white elements woven at same time. Warp pattern technique, presentable only on one side; thus not considered a tapestry of the highest class. Warp: cotton, three "kettles." Weft (makes pattern): wool from llama and vicuna.

Figure 118:   "Brocade" of red, gold, beige and white. Stripes show direction of weft. Extra wefts were added for the intricate interlocking bird motif rows.

                   Warp "floats" behind the material when it is not incorporated into the front design, making a thick cloth. The selvages in the horizontal indicate its original width, but its length is unknown.

tall hats, like NWC potlatch hats, indicate prestige

slant eyes—perhaps mystical sign
earplugs and ear ornaments

monkey, guardian creature
(matching monkey broken off)

119.   Single spout vessel, two views.[3]
        Post-proto Chimu, 1200 A.D.
        Pacasmayo site, Moché Valley, Peru.
        Clay, 6", red-burned-gray.
        AIAI.
        Original colors may have been red
and white.

on handle, a
reclining figure,
probably a slave

pedestal with stamped design

120. **Effigy vessel.**
Late Chimu, 1300 A.D.
Moché Valley, near Trujillo, Peru (north coast).
Clay, 10", smoked black gray.
Original paint may have been black, orange and white.
AIAI.

Both of the single spout effigy vases (Figs. 119 and 120) are from Pacasmayo in northern Peru and probably date from 1200—1300 A.D.* The vases are used to contain ashes after cremation. At the base of the spout, on both figures, the solemn faces with long, slanted eyes are of ceremonial significance, representing in effigy either the deceased person, a warrior, or a mythological figure.** Compare the incised eye lines and dots with those of the Great Idol diagram, Fig. 92.

The pots were made in two stages. First a slab of clay was pressed into a mold—a process by which many similar vessels could be quickly turned out. Once the piece was removed from the mold, a "stamp" design was pressed into the pedestal to form a repeated pattern. Then, more than likely, the pot was painted, though the color has since reverted to natural clay. The mold technique was developed around the first century A.D.; the "stamp" idea came later. Artisans in Morrope, a village northwest of Pacasmayo, still work in a similar tradition.[4]

---

* The burial site which contained the two vases was discovered during the construction of a motel.

** The familiar motif of a figure flanked by two animals. See pp. 28 and 32.

121. Chinese Thunder motif "Lei-wen."
Clay pot.
Ma Chang period, 1700–1300 B.C.
Kansu, China.

The spiral motif is common to most primitive cultures, with some minor variations. In the mummy bundle (Fig. 118, section F), the spiral is squared while in section C it is rounded slightly.

The squared version is basically referred to as a **fret hook.** It can be seen in the very early Chinese pot (Fig. 121, 1700 B.C.) and in a Mexican rug (Fig. 122). Cultures from both Peru and Mexico combine or lock the background in with the spiral motif to form a black positive and white negative fret hook.* Such interchangeability is possible only in a flat design.

The rounded spiral is seen in Fig. 116, from the Mayan Culture, as well as on the preceding Shang (1500 B.C.) Chinese items, Figs. 15 and 69. It is an extremely popular motif of the Maoris, of some New Guinea cultures, and of the Amur River cultures of Eastern Asia.

Among Northwest Coast tribes the spiral motif is used to indicate the nostrils of the bear and beaver. Most of the space filler motifs (Fig. 11) consist of equidistant curves. The "eye" is a double circle, and the "wing tip" a triple enclosure; these, like the spiral designs, help to break up large surfaces, and seem closely akin to the spiral. Each encloses a white circle.

---

* A technique intriguingly used by M. C. Escher in lithographs and woodcuts, and recently enjoying a revival in popularity.

122. **Fret-hook diagonal-step motif (Zapotec Design) blanket.**
San Miguel de Allende, Mexico, 1950.
Cotton. AIAI.

Here the fret-hook is combined with the stop-block to form a simple bold motif. This right-angle design seems naturally adapted to weaving or twining techniques with their limited straight-grid construction. This design is referred to as "light worm," *xonecuille.* It is used on the interior wall at the Zapotec Palace at Mitla, Oaxaca, Mexico, (300 A.D.).

123. **Storage basket of step-block (lightning) motif.**
Lillooet, Coast Salish, Northwest Coast, 1925.
H. 11", w. 17", d. 10½" (at top).
Cedar bark, fern stems, spruce splinters.

step-block motif

ACKNOWLEDGMENTS

The original impetus for this work came from our association with the **Alaska International Art Institute** and with its art collection, which provides a meaningful framework for the book. We hope that the book, in turn, has provided a coherent interpretation of a portion of the collection. **H. Wendy Jones,** founder of the Institute, has offered much encouragement in this project, including assumption of publication costs.

Among those who have read and helpfully criticized various drafts of this work are: Meg Fritz, David Hatch, and Joseph A. Hester. Constructive comments on various aspects of the work were made by Dorothy Menzel, Moises Roizen, Ann Rowe, John H. Rowe and Philip Welch. Special thanks go to Novella Simonson for significant editorial assistance rendered unstintingly just when needed.

ILLUSTRATIONS

The Protruding Tongue

X-ray Views

The Joint Mark as Decoration and Visual Metaphor

A Union of Bird and Man

Fig. 76   Man-eagle design on food basin, Anasazi, New Mexico; Smithsonian Institution, Washington, D.C.; Covarrubias, 1954, Fig. 68.

Fig. 77   Man-eagle shield design, Zuni, Arizona; litho. by T. Sinclair & Son; Frank H. Cushing, *Zuni Fetishes.*

Fig. 78   Bird protecting a human being, bronze emblem, western Siberia; Fraser, 1966, p. 290.

Fig. 79   Ptarmigan hunting mask, Eskimo; Courtesy of the Brooklyn Museum. Acc. no. 44.34.7.

Fig. 80   *"Swaixwe"* mask, Salish, Northwest Coast; Courtesy of the American Museum of Natural History, New York, cat. #319751.

Fig. 81   Bird and man drum, Sepik River, New Guinea; British Museum; Schmitz, 1962, plate 7.

Fig. 82   Sea Monster mask, Kwakuitl, Northwest Coast; Cape Mudge, B.C., Canada; Museum of the American Indian; Courtesy of Museum of the American Indian, Heye Foundation, no. 10/254.

Fig. 83   Bird-man mask used in *malanggan* ceremonies, New Ireland. Courtesy of Museum of Cultural History, UCLA, no. 64-3951.

Fig. 84   Thunderbird—human mask, Kwakiutl, Northwest Coast; Courtesy of the American Museum of Natural History, New York, #315407.

Fig. 85   Transformation mask, human figure with *inua,* Eskimo; United States National Museum, #64260. Fraser, 1966, Fig. 15, p. 292.

Fig. 86   "After Fishing," painting by Rusty Heurlin; AIAI. Photograph by Thomas Flower.

Totem Poles

Fig. 87   Photo, "Masked Kwakiutl Dancers," by Edward S. Curtis, 1915. Courtesy of Museum of Northern British Columbia, Prince Rupert, B.C., Canada.

Fig. 88   Raven Totem by William Jeffrey, Tsimshian, Northwest Coast, Two views; AIAI; Photographs by Thomas Flower.

Fig. 89   "Raven and the Daughter of the Nass," woodcut by Dale de Armond, Juneau, Alaska, 1963; AIAI.

Fig. 90   Cenotaph of a Tiki, Maori, New Zealand, Raroera Pak, sketch by K. Bigwood, from *The New Zealander Illustrated,* G. F. Angas, London, 1846, in *Terence Barrow, The Decorative Arts of the New Zealand Maori,* p. 81.

Fig. 91   Ruler or raingod, stele, Mayan Culture. Photo by A. F. Maudslay, 1885 in G. H. S. Bushnell, *Ancient Arts of the Americas,* p. 107.

FOOTNOTES

(Please consult Bibliography, pp. 124 — 127, for complete information as to title and author.)

Artistic Similarities Between Cultures: Some Theories

1.   Levi-Strauss, p. 248.
2.   Levi-Strauss, p. 258.
3.   Levi-Strauss, p. 265.

The Northwest Coast Indians

1.   Hawthorne (1967), p. 152.
2.   Daugherty, "The Ozette Archaeological Expedition."
3.   Inverarity, p. 30.
4.   Gunther, *Art in the Life of the Northwest Coast Indians,* p. 113.
5.   Netting, p. 10.
6.   Gunther, *op. cit.,* p. 113.
7.   Netting, p. 10.
8.   Gunther, *op. cit.,* p. 7.

Design Principles: Handling Space

1.   Gunther, *op. cit.,* p. 6.
2.   Gunther, *op. cit.,* p. 7.
3.   Emmons, "The Chilkat Blanket."
4.   Perceval Yetts, quoted in Bowenhamp, p. 47.
5.   Interpretation of pictograph derived from personal communication from Tatiana Proskouriakoff, Peabody Museum, Harvard University.
6.   Bernal.

The Figure Split and Splayed

1.   Fraser, p. 57.
2.   Fraser, p. 48.
3.   Fraser, p. 73.
4.   Barrow (1969).

A Union of Bird and Reptile

1.   Badner, p. 20.
2.   Locher, p. 10.
3.   Fraser, p. 57.
4.   Deborah Waite, "Kwakiutl Transformation Masks," in Fraser, p. 266.
5.   Deborah Waite, in Fraser, p. 283.
6.   Nelson, p. 487.

Double-Headed Serpents

1.   Ralph Coe, p. 85.
2.   Nelson, p. 444–445.
3.   Bowenhamp, p. 17.
4.   Ralph Coe, pp. 86–87.
5.   Inverarity, p. 17.

The Protruding Tongue

1. Badner, p. 40.
2. Badner, p. 22.
3. Barrow (1969), p. 18.
4. Barrow (1969), p. 21.

The Joint Mark as Decoration and Visual Metaphor

1. Barrow (1964), plates 2 and 37.
2. Fraser, p. 42, and Barrow (1969), p. 19.
3. Bowenhamp, p. 65.
4. Fraser, p. 78.
5. Flügel, chapters xii and xiii.
6. Barrow (1964), p. 8.
7. Barrow (1964), p. 66.
8. Frog legend derived from personal communication from Ester Billman, Curator, Sheldon Jackson Museum, Sitka, Alaska.
9. See "Eskimo Cultures," *Encyclopedia of World Art,* Vol. 5, Plate 2, 1962.

A Union of Bird and Man

1. Barbeau, p. 202.
2. Barbeau, p. 200.
3. Garfield, p. 63.
4. Barrow (1969), pp. 56—67.
5. Hoover, pp. 1—26.
6. Keeler, pp. 59—96.
7. Cushing, pp. 41—42.
8. Fraser.
9. Badner, p. 52.
10. Badner, p. 60.
11. Levi-Strauss, p. 262.
12. Badner, p. 53.
13. Nelson, p. 365.

Totem Poles

1. Legend adapted from personal communication with Mr. William Jeffrey.
2. Barbeau, p. 263.
3. Bowenhamp, p. 46.
4. NWC Raven legend adapted from Inverarity, p. 33.
5. Eskimo Raven legend adapted from Nelson, pp. 460—462.
6. Michael D. Coe, personal communication.
7. Most interpretive information presented here on Stele D is derived from Morley, *Guide Book to the Ruins of Quirigua.*
8. Gardner, p. 595.
9. Interpretation of the Great Idol of Tiahuanaco is derived from Posnansky, *Tiahuanacu: The Cradle of American Man,* Vol. 1.
10. Bellamy (1956), Indroduction.

11. Barbeau, p. 202.
12. Legend of Wackhayea adapted from personal communication with Mr. William Jeffrey.
13. Illustrated in Badner.
14. Bowenhamp.
15. Rua legend adapted from Barrow (1969), p. 23.
16. Barrow (1969), p. 23.

The Burial Context

1. Levi-Strauss, p. 260.
2. Much of the weaving information pertaining to the textile fragments was supplied by Ann Rowe, The Textile Museum, Washington, D.C.
3. The single spout vessel, Fig. 119, is almost an exact replica of one illustrated in Fig. h, Plate 67, Kroeber and Lowie.
4. Donald Collier, "Pottery Stamping and Molding on the North Coast of Peru," in Rowe and Menzel, p. 264.

INDEX OF ITEMS BY CULTURE

124. TIME—CULTURE CORRELATION CHART

	North America	Mexico	Central America	South America	South Seas	China	Japan	Siberia
7000—1500 BC						Yang—Shao Ma-chang		
1500—1000 BC		Chiapas				Shang		
1000—500 BC	Old Bering Sea					Chou		
500 BC — 1 AD	Old Bering Sea							
1 — 500 AD	Old Bering Sea, Wakashan Culture, Northwest Coast	Vera-cruz Monte Alban III	Nicoya Peninsula, Costa Rica	Paracas Tiahua-naco, Peru				
500—1000 AD	Mimbres Late Anasazi		Mayan					
1000—1500 AD	Navajo Modern Eskimo	Toltec Aztec	Coclé Panama	Chimu Lambay-eque Valley, Peru Reventazon	New Ireland Maori Papua New Hebrides Indonesia			
1500—2000 AD	Modern Northwest Coast Zuni, Ariz.	Aztec	Cuna Panama		Marquesas Isles		Ainu	Siberia

BIBLIOGRAPHY

Anton, Ferdinand; and Frederick J. Dockstader, *Pre-Columbian Art and Later Indian Tribal Arts,* Abrams, Inc. New York, 1968. pp. 35, 112, 159, 180, 198.

Badner, Mino, "The Protruding Tongue Motif in the Sculpture of the Northwest Coast of America," Master of Arts thesis, Columbia University, 1963.

Barbeau, Marius, *Haida Myths Illustrated in Argillite Carvings.* Bulletin 127, Anthropological Series No. 32, Department of Resources and Development, National Parks Branch, National Museum of Canada.

Barrow, Terry, *The Decorative Arts of the New Zealand Maori,* A. H. and A. W. Reed, Wellington, 1964.

Barrow, Terry, *Maori Wood Sculpture of New Zealand.* Chas. E. Tuttle Co., Tokyo, 1969.

Bellamy, H. S., and P. Allan, *The Calendar of Tiahuanaco: A Disquisition on the Time Measuring System of the Oldest Civilization in the World.* London. Faber & Faber Ltd., 1956.

Bellamy, H. S. and P. Allan, *The Great Idol of Tiahuanaco, An Interpretation in the Light of the Hoerbiger Theory of Satellites of the Glyphs Carved on Its Surface.* Faber and Faber, London, 1959.

Bernal, Ignacio, *3000 Years of Art and Life in Mexico As Seen in the National Museum of Anthropology with Roman Pina-Chan and Fernando Camara-Barbachano;* translated by Caroline Czitron. Abrams, Inc., New York, 1968.

Bird, Junius, and Louisa Bellinger, *The Textile Museum: Paracas Fabrics and Nazca Needlework.* National Publishing Company, Washington, D. C., 1954.

Boas, Franz, *Primitive Art,* Dover Pub. Inc., New York, 1955. pp. 1–373.

Bowenhamp, Lynne, et al., *Early Chinese Art and the Pacific Basin, A Photographic Exhibition,* with introduction by Douglas Fraser. Columbia University, New York, 1967.

Buehler, Alfred; Terry Barron; and Charles P. Mountford, *The Art of the South Sea Islands Including Australia and New Zealand.* Crown Publishers, Inc., New York, 1962.

Burland, Cottie , *North American Indian Mythology.* Tudor Publishing Company, New York, 1965. pp. 1–152.

Bushnell, G. H. S., *Ancient Arts of the Americas.* F. A. Praeger, New York, 1965. pp. 140–142, 45–48, 88, 106.

Coe, Ralph T., "Asiatic Sources of Northwest Coast Art," *American Indian Art: Form and Tradition.* E. P. Dutton and Co., Inc., New York, 1972. pp. 85–92.

Covarrubias, Miguel, *The Eagle, the Jaguar, and the Serpent: Indian Art of the Americas; North America: Alaska, Canada, the United States.* Knopf, New York, 1954. pp. 3–314.

Cushing, Frank H., *Zuni Fetishes* (Bureau of Ethnology, 2nd Annual Report 1881). K. C. Publications, Las Vegas, Nevada, 1966.

Daugherty, Richard D., "The Ozette Archaeological Expedition," Washington State University. (Pamphlet).

De Minil, Adelaide (photographs) and William Reid (text), *Out of Silence*, published for Amon Carter Museum, Fort Worth, by Outerbridge and Dienstfrey, New York, 1971.

Emmons, George T., "The Chilkat Blanket," *Memoirs of the Museum of Natural History, Vol. III, Part IV;* with notes on blanket designs by Franz Boas. The Knickerbocker Press, New York, 1907.

Flügel, J. C., *The Psycho-Analytic Study of the Family* ("The International Psycho-Analytical Library," No. 3, 4th edition.) The Hogarth Press, London, 1931.

Fraser, Douglas, "The Heraldic Woman: A Study in Diffusion" (1965); and Deborah Waite, "Kwakiutl Transformation Masks" (1964); from *The Many Faces of Primitive Art, a Critical Anthology,* ed. Douglas Fraser. Prentice-Hall, Inc., Englewood Cliffs, New Jersey, 1966.

Gardner, Helen, *Art Through the Ages,* fourth edition, revised under the editorship of Sumner McK. Crosby by The Department of the History of Art, Yale University. Harcourt, Brace & World, Inc., New York, 1959.

Garfield, Viola E., and Linn A. Forrest, *The Wolf and the Raven.* University of Washington Press, Seattle, 1948. pp. 1–151.

Guiart, Jean, *The Arts of the South Pacific* (Translated by Anthony Christie), a part of the series, *The Arts of Mankind,* edited by Andre Malraux and Georges Salles. Thames and Hudson, London, 1963.

Gunther, Erna, *Northwest Coast Indian Art.* A catalog from the Seattle Centennial 21 Exposition, 1966.

Gunther, Erna, *Art in the Life of the Northwest Coast Indians.* Published by the Portland Art Museum, Portland, Oregon, 1966.

Hawthorne, Audrey, *Art of the Kwakiutl Indians,* University of British Columbia, Vancouver, 1967.

Hawthorne, Audrey, *People of the Potlatch: Native Arts and Culture of the Pacific Northwest Coast.* Vancouver Art Gallery with the University of British Columbia. No date. pp. 7–109.

Hoover, F. Louis, *Molas from the San Blas Islands.* Art Gallery, Center for Inter-American Relations, New York, 1968. pp. 1–26

Huyghe, René, (ed.), translated by Heron, Lambert and Schurmann, *Art and Mankind: Larousse Encyclopedia of Prehistoric and Ancient Art.* Prometheus Press, New York, 1962.

Inverarity, Robert Bruce, *Art of the Northwest Coast Indians.* Berkeley, University of California Press, 1950. pp. 1–243.

Keeler, Clyde E., *Cuna Indian Art: The Culture and Craft of Panama's San Blas Islanders.* Exposition Press, Jericho, New York, 1969. pp. 59–96.

Kuh, Katharine, "Alaska's Vanishing Art," *Saturday Review,* Oct. 22, 1966. pp. 25–31.

Kroeber, A. L. and Robert H. Lowie (eds.), *University of California Publications in American Archaeology and Ethnology, Vol. XXI,* 1924–1927, Berkeley, Calif.

Levi-Strauss, Claude, *Structural Anthropology;* translated by Claire Jacobson and Brooke Grundfest Schoepf. Basic Books, Inc., New York, 1963.

Locher, G. W., *The Serpent in Kwakiutl Religion.* Leiden: E. J. Brill, 1932.

Lothrop, Samuel Kirkland, et al., *Essays in Pre-Columbian Art and Archaeology.* Harvard University Press, Cambridge, Mass., 1961.

Lothrop, Samuel Kirkland, et al. *Memoirs of the Peabody Museum of Archaeology and Ethnology, Harvard University, Vol. VII.* "Coclé, An Archaeological Study of Central Panama," Peabody Museum, Cambridge, Part I, 1937; Vol. VIII, Part II, 1942.

Maudslay, A. P., *Biologia Centrali-Americana; or, Contributions to the Knowledge of the Fauna and Flora of Mexico and Central America: Archaeology, Vol. II* (Plates); eds. F. Ducane Godman and Osbert Salvin. R. H. Porter, pub., London, 1899–1902.

Michael, Henry N., Ed., *Anthropology of the North: Translations from Russian Sources. The Archaeology and Geomorphology of Northern Asia: Selected Works No. 5.* pp. 296–348.
Arutyunov, S.A.; Levin, M.G.; Sergeyev, D.A., "Ancient Burials on the Chukchi Peninsula," University of Toronto Press, 1964, Canada.

Montandon, George, *La Civilisation Ainon, et les Cultures Artiques,* Payont, Paris, 1937. pp. 80, 225.

Morley, Sylvanus, *Guide Book to the Ruins of Quirigua.* Washington, D.C., Carnegie Institution of Washington (Supplementary Publication No. 16), 1935.

Nelson, Edward William, *The Eskimo About Bering Strait, Eighteenth Annual Report of The Bureau of American Ethnology, 1899.*

Netting, Robert McC., *The Ecological Approach in Cultural Study,* a McCaleb Module in Anthropology from the series Addison-Wesley Modular Publications. March 6, 1971. pp. 8–12.

Poignant, Roslyn, *Oceanic Mythology: The Myths of Polynesia, Micronesia, Melanesia, Australia.* Paul Hamlin, Ltd., Drury House, London. 1967. pp. 1–140.

Posnansky, Arthur, *Tiahuanacu: The Cradle of American Man, Vol. 1;* translated by James F. Shearer. J. J. Augustin, New York, 1945. pp. 70–115.

Rowe, John H., and Dorothy Menzel, *Peruvian Archaeology, Selected Readings.* Peck Publications, Palo Alto, Calif., 1967.

Rice, Tamara Talbot, *Ancient Arts of Central Asia.* Frederick T. Praeger, 1965. pp. 11–54.

Schmitz, Carl A., *The Acanthus History of Sculpture: Oceanic Sculpture,* Sir Herbert Read and H. D. Molesworth, eds. New York Graphic Society, Connecticut, 1962.

Wardwell, Allen, *Yakutat South—Indian Art of the Northwest Coast.* The Art Institute of Chicago, Hillison & Allen Company, Chicago, 1964. pp. 1–80.